Addiction-Free

How to Help an Alcoholic or
Addict Get Started on Recovery

Also by Gene Hawes

*Rx for Recovery: The Medical and Health Guide for Alcoholics,
Addicts, and Their Families* (with Jeffrey Weisberg, M.D.)

Childbearing: A Book of Choices (with Dr. Ruth Watson Lubic)

The Career-Changer's Sourcebook

The College Board Guide to Going to College While Working

The Encyclopedia of Second Careers

Hawes on Getting into College

Hawes Guide to Successful Study Skills (with Lynne S. Hawes)

Hawes Comprehensive Guide to Colleges

The Complete Career Guide (with David M. Brownstone)

Careers Tomorrow: Leading Growth Fields for College Graduates

The New American Guide to Colleges

How to Get College Scholarships

*To Advance Knowledge: A Handbook on American
University Press Publishing*

Educational Testing for the Millions

Addiction-Free

*How to Help an Alcoholic or
Addict Get Started on Recovery*

Gene Hawes

and

Anderson Hawes

Thomas Dunne Books
St. Martin's Press 📖 *New York*

THOMAS DUNNE BOOKS.
An imprint of St. Martin's Press.

www.stmartins.com

Library of Congress Cataloging-in-Publication Data

Hawes, Gene R.
    Addiction-free : how to help an alcoholic or drug addict get started on recovery / Gene Hawes and Anderson Hawes.—1st ed.
        p. cm.
    Includes bibliographical references.
    ISBN 0-312-25182-3 (hc)
    ISBN 0-312-31111-7 (pbk)
    1. Substance Abuse—Treatment. 2. Addicts—Rehabilitation.
    I. Hawes, Anderson. II. Title

HV4998 .H39 2001
362.29'18—dc21   2001042402

First St. Martin's Griffin Edition: January 2003

10 9 8 7 6 5 4 3 2 1

To the late A. Eugene Hawes,

who started on his recovery in 1940

through the way of chapter 1

Contents

Contents

Acknowledgments

A great many members of Alcoholics Anonymous provided invaluable information for this book in discussions with the authors and at Open Meetings of AA. Their contributions, to chapter 1 especially, remain anonymous ones out of respect for the fundamental AA tradition of anonymity for its living members. Their help is greatly appreciated. Even more, we are glad to be able to help carry their message.

Extremely important suggestions for improving the book were made by Eliot and Leda Fremont-Smith, who read portions of the manuscript while it was being written. As a result, the book benefits both from their knowledge as professional substance abuse counselors and from their encouragement as treasured friends.

Especially powerful insights into clinical and medical aspects of alcoholism and addiction are reflected in the book through prior work of Gene Hawes with Jeffrey Weisberg, M.D., of Continuum Health Partners, Inc., in New York City. (Continuum Health Partners is the parent corporation of Beth Israel Medical Center, St. Luke's-Roosevelt Hospital Center, Long Island College Hospital, and New York Eye and Ear Infirmary.) Dr. Weisberg and Mr. Hawes are the authors of *Rx for Recovery: The Medical and Health Guide for Alcoholics, Addicts, and Their Families.*

Extensive research for the content of the section "Sources of Help and Information" (page 193) was provided by Michael H. DeBellis. His enthusiasm as well as his formidable skills helped mightily.

Acknowledgments

More than anyone, Thomas Dunne made the book possible. We can hardly begin to thank him enough.

Anderson Hawes wishes to thank the following people for their contributions:

Tim Rice, M.D., A.S.A.M., Medical Director of the Community Health Center, Inc., and Associate Medical Director of Education of Ignatia Hall in Akron, Ohio, kindly reviewed the medical information pertaining to detoxification signs and symptoms in chapter 2.

Margaret Mattson, Ph.D., of the National Institute on Alcohol Abuse and Alcoholism (NIAAA), shared valuable research on Project Match.

Anita Gadzuk of the Office of Applied Studies at the Department of Health and Human Services, Substance Abuse and Mental Health Services Administration, assisted in providing access and guidance to current research publications and data sources.

Colleagues Thomas E. Pickton, Ph.D., James Siddall, Ph.D., Janet Wagner, and Ted Ziegler, have provided ongoing support, and their contributions to the field of substance abuse treatment emphasize the care and treatment of affected family members.

My wife, Lisa, and my two children, Tyler and Mason, helped immeasurably with their patience and understanding of yet another project.

Introduction

Some person in your life has probably started to worry you—and worry you pretty badly. In a worst case, he or she is someone terribly important to you, such as

- your husband or your wife, or your lover or life-partner;
- your dad or your mom (or both!);
- your brother or sister;
- your daughter or son—or your grandchild;
- your granddad or your grandmother;
- a key employee; or
- a wonderful friend.

Little by little, that person has changed. He or she has let you down more and more—unpredictably. At times, that person may have seemed dazed, confused, and alarmingly different. You've seen many signs that the person might be drinking alcohol or taking drugs uncontrollably. The person has probably been uncomfortably evasive or angry, or has perhaps made excuses whenever you've questioned him or her about the drug use or drinking.

Other times, the person may have convinced you that your worries are unfounded. Or the person may have sworn that he or she would never let it happen again. Maybe you've been shouted at or told to butt out and mind your own business.

$$\Big[\begin{array}{c} \textbf{One Drinker in Every Eight} \\ \textbf{Is an Alcoholic or an Addict} \end{array} \Big]$$

If someone you care about is putting you through worry and pain, you're not alone—far from it. Two-thirds of all Americans age twelve and up drink at least some alcohol every year—about 140 million women and men. And of those, some 18 million are alcoholics.[1]

What does this mean? Think of the last time you were at any kind of party with drinks, or when you last visited a bar or cocktail lounge. One in every eight women and men you saw there is an alcoholic, on the average. It also means that you'd find one alcoholic in about every fifth nuclear family in America, on average. But because alcoholism often runs in families, a family predisposed to the disease will typically have more than one alcoholic.

Something like 26 million Americans a year also use illegal drugs. Drugs like cocaine, crack cocaine, heroin, speed, LSD, marijuana. And 5.5 million of these Americans have become addicted to drugs badly enough to need treatment, according to estimates by the National Academy of Sciences.[2] Women and men also become addicted to habit-forming prescription drugs—such potent painkillers as Percodan, Percocet, Hycodan, Demerol, Dilaudid or morphine, and sedatives like Seconal or Nembutal, or tranquilizers like Valium.

Often, drug addicts of all these types now overlap with the alcohol addicts. These days, it has become more and more common for addicts in early and middle adult years to be addicted to drugs and alcohol interchangeably. Either separately or together, alcohol addiction and drug addiction affect Americans in epidemic proportions.

Introduction

[**Addiction Fights Off Treatment**]

The problem posed by the addiction of someone in your life can be enormous in personal terms. Addiction to alcohol or drugs has won complete recognition as a disease. Medical scientists and clinicians often professionally term it chemical dependence or substance abuse. Physicians can now become certified in the treatment of addiction as a subspecialty of internal medicine. Federal Medicaid and Medicare programs—and commonly health insurance plans—authorize coverage for treatment expenses.

However, few diseases wreak such havoc on their victims—and on those involved with the victims, like yourself. People who suffer from most other diseases get diagnoses and treatment as soon as possible, and show enormous gratitude to all those who help them recognize and recover from their afflictions.

But addiction leads its sufferers to deny—more and more vehemently as time goes on—that they have a disease and to turn against anyone who tries to help. Meanwhile, the addicts deteriorate physically. Emotionally, they become malicious and hateful. They often lie and steal as their addiction dictates, and they blame everyone and everything else for what's happening. Family life with them becomes a living hell—as you may know. They often have acute money problems, serious accidents, and illnesses. In time, they become unable to do almost anything. But the decline to utter catastrophe may unfold gradually, over many excruciatingly painful years.

[**Their Addiction Can Hurt or Kill You**]

The closer you are to the addict in your life, the greater your risk of harm. Someone else's addiction could even kill you: for instance, almost four out of every ten fatal auto accidents in the United States involve alcohol. And alcohol is a factor in most of the violent crimes that lead to jail terms.

Financially, you can be seriously harmed by being involved with an alcoholic/addict. In time, alcoholics/addicts irresistibly lose all earnings and savings, and they must do whatever it takes to get money for their addiction from those around them. This can go on until you have virtually nothing left.

It's very likely, too, that you'll deny the growing addiction of the addict in your life as much as the addict does. So fervently do the addicts believe their own excuses that their families and friends believe them, too. Sadly, the more you care about the addict, the more you want to believe.

"But I was under so much pressure."

"I absolutely won't ever do it again."

"You'd do it too if you had to put up with a job like mine."

"The children were so awfully difficult today."

"I just needed to calm my nerves."

"If you'd had a day like mine, you'd understand."

As you accept excuses like the ones above, you become torn over whether the booze and drug crises are just one-time, isolated events, or if they are, in fact, part of a pattern. You find yourself lying to others to cover up for your alcoholic/addict, and you believe the need for the lies if not the lies themselves. You come to live in constant terror over when the next crisis or blowup will strike. You seethe with towering rage at the hurts inflicted by your alcoholic/ addict; then you reproach yourself for jumping to conclusions and imagining that things are worse than they really are.

In the most dangerous scenario, you become as blind to the addiction as the alcoholic/addict is—and almost as badly warped.

[Two Problems: Yours and the Addict's]

As a result, if you're closely involved with the alcoholic/addict, you face not only the problem of getting the addict into recovery, but you also need to get yourself into recovery. For your own sake especially (but also for the sake of the addict), it's best if you can get into recovery first.

And recovery begins with recognition: with accepting the disease of addiction for what it really is, with seeing what damage it has done, and with understanding how much more damage it will cause unless stopped.

But take heart. You have already embarked on your recovery by reading this far and recognizing your predicament here.

• *Solving Your Problem with Addiction*

Your problem with the addiction of someone in your life stems from the torturous and deeply ingrained, habitual ways you have been forced to adapt to the disease. Those painful, habitual reactions and emotions will almost certainly go on unless you begin to identify and change them—even if the addict and the addiction were somehow to disappear completely from your life.

Your recovery will be the more difficult the more closely involved you've been with the alcoholic/addict. It can be rather hard even if your connection to the alcoholic/addict is fairly modest, perhaps consisting of a work relationship or a casual friendship.

Learning the basic truths about alcoholism/addiction will be your first important task. Those precepts are set forth mainly in the introduction and in chapter 1. Knowing those truths will enable you to recognize them in the addict in your life. Further steps to your recovery are explained primarily in chapter 3, "The Al-Anon Way."

Addiction generates a downward spiral—a giant whirlpool of misery and ruin—in the lives of the addict and everyone around the addict. But recovery generates an upward spiral. Pursuing your own recovery improves your life even if it has no effect on the alcoholic/addict. Your progress can even prove to be one of the most powerful forces to move the addict into her or his own recovery.

• *Solving the Alcoholic's/Addict's Problem of Addiction*

You have many very powerful sources of help for getting your alcoholic/addict into recovery, especially once you begin the process yourself. Among them are organizations of literally millions of former alcoholics/addicts worldwide, who are in recovery and who help others to get into recovery cost-free. Among them are thousands of treatment centers and programs nationwide, which are operated by the medical and other health-care professions. Also among them are potent practices of police and the courts, as well as employer-sponsored programs that effectively identify and then help addicted employees to start on recovery.

The rest of this book explains all these sources of help for you and for the alcoholic/addict in your life. One or more of them should provide the key to solving the problem of addiction for your alcoholic/addict. They already have done so for millions of alcoholics/addicts with problems absolutely as bad as yours or even far worse.

[Great Rewards Ahead for You]

Right now, your life with an alcoholic/addict is likely to feel terribly black, fearful, and enraged. However, believe this: you have every reason for hope. First, pursuing your own recovery can free you of most of the misery of your own life, regardless of when the addict may get into recovery. Second, striving to get your alcoholic/addict into recovery often is nothing less than a matter of life and death. Alcoholism/addiction unchecked leads many sufferers to insanity and death. Your efforts could also prevent years of misery and ruin in addition to saving a life.

Moreover, many women and men recovering from alcoholism/ addiction find that life in recovery holds satisfactions, and even joys, they had never dreamed of before.

[*Prologue*]

Sure Signs of the Disease
of Alcoholism/Addiction

Y*ou need to* apply *outside* guidelines impartially to start getting better yourself if someone close to you seems to be heading into alcoholism/addiction. Steel yourself to find out the worst.

Remember: Alcoholism/addiction can strike *anywhere*. You may at first feel that alcoholism/addiction just can't happen among your family or friends or in your company. But it can and does strike anywhere. No amount of fame or wealth or success can guarantee safety.

Even presidents of the United States have had alcoholism/addiction strike very close in recent years. For example Bill Clinton's younger half-brother, Roger Clinton, became a cocaine addict and was convicted as a drug dealer.[1] The brother of President Jimmy Carter, Billy Carter, developed alcoholism and entered recovery.[2]

In the White House itself, First Lady Betty Ford, wife of President Gerald Ford, suffered increasingly from alcoholism and addiction to prescription drugs. Shortly after her husband left office, she agreed to try treatment. (The type of treatment used for her is described in chapter 2.)

So moved were she and her family by her experience that she went on to found what has become one of the nation's best-known centers for treating alcoholism/addiction, the world-renowned Betty Ford Center in Rancho Mirage, California.[3]

Presidential candidate and former Senator George McGovern and his family went through an agonizing battle to save his daughter Teresa from the ravages of alcoholism/addiction. After a first onslaught of the disease, she managed an unbroken eight years in sober recovery. But after she went into a bar and got drunk one bitterly cold winter night, she collapsed in the snow behind a print shop and froze to death.[4]

Bill Moyers, former presidential press secretary and the celebrated creator and host of TV documentaries, was similarly moved by shattering experience with alcoholism/addiction in his immediate family. That experience with his son led Moyers to produce a four-hour documentary on alcoholism/addiction, which was broadcast over national public TV in 1999.

Many highly successful celebrities in wide varieties of fields have also been stricken with alcoholism/addiction. Here are a few examples: authors Susan Cheever, Erica Jong, and Elmore Leonard; baseball stars Darryl Strawberry and Bob Welch; actors Rod Steiger, Chevy Chase, Carrie Fisher, and Mary Tyler Moore; television producer Barbara Gordon; star ballerina Gelsey Kirkland; and TV anchorman Jim Jensen.

No amount of success or acclaim or wealth can make those close to you immune to the disease of alcoholism/addiction.

[Can You Arrest Alcoholism/Addiction Early?]

You may wonder whether you might be able to head off a loved one's developing alcoholism/addiction by responding to the person's needs early. It's possible that you have seen early warning signs. These might include very occasional failures of responsibility because the individual was intoxicated with liquor and/or drugs (or because of a subsequent hangover).

Failures like these are a major sign and an increasingly disastrous consequence of alcoholism/addiction: failure to get to work on time—or to go to work at all; failure to make important business meetings, such as job interviews, sales appointments, conferences with the boss or supervisor; failures to go to class in school or college; failure to show up for exams; failure to do important things for one's children (such as attend scheduled teacher's conferences, plays, sports matches, or even birthday parties and graduations). Eventually, the addict may even fail to get washed or showered or dressed or fed.

• *Try to Stop Addiction Early*
Suppose a person in your life drinks or takes drugs rather often and sometimes heavily. Suppose, too, that the person has no history of ignoring his or her responsibilities. But you've noticed in recent months or weeks that the person isn't meeting his or her obligations, as a result of drinking or drugging, or both. Your faimily member or friend could be headed for full-blown addiction.

On the chance that he or she actually *is* on that trajectory, you could try to help. Set aside a time to talk to her or him privately and without interruption. Tell the person very seriously how concerned you are about where he or she may be heading. Suggest a complete stop to the use of any alcohol or drugs. You might suggest that the person could be casual about this change with friends and associates and need only say that the drinking or drugging has caused stomach upsets, so stopping seems worth a try.

You'd be very lucky if this should work.

• Early Arrest May Not Head Off Addiction

You need to know certain basic facts about the disease of alcoholism/addiction in order to understand what your chances of success are with such an early intercession.

First, some people have an inherent physical potential to become alcoholics or addicts. To a large extent, this potential has been found to be inherited. For example, studies have shown that the children of alcoholic parents are about *four times more likely* to become alcoholics than the children of nonalcoholic parents.

Many persons who lack this natural potential can drink alcohol for years—in some cases, even heavily—and never become alcoholics. Such people can and do quit drinking if they really need to—for reasons as varied as stopping serious liver damage caused by alcohol, holding on to their job, or keeping a lover or a spouse.

Quite a few Americans (some studies suggest as many as one out of every ten) have this inborn predisposition to alcoholism. But in order for them to become alcoholics, they must activate their potential by drinking substantially for some time—often, for a few years at least.

• Possible Success

Now, let's apply these facts to a possible attempt to head off alcoholism early in someone close to you. Consider first the cases in

4

which you might be successful. Assume that the person could be merely a careless heavy drinker who does not have the physical potential for alcoholism. People like this should stop without much difficulty if convinced that their drinking seriously interferes with their well-being.

Then, too, you could be far more successful if the person does have the inborn tendencies—but has not been drinking long enough to activate that potential for alcoholism. Should this be the case, the person would still have the ability to stop if you and the circumstances were convincing enough.

• *Your Worst Case*

Your worst case, on the other hand, would be one in which the person whom you want much to help has the inherited addictive potential and has gone on drinking long enough to activate irreversible alcoholism. Your attempt with such a person would come too late. It's possible that you might at first think you had succeeded—if the person initially misled you, as well as herself or himself. The person might even stop drinking for some weeks or months to prove there's no problem. (Some alcoholics/addicts do just this, for reassurance.)

But sooner or later, people with alcoholism revert to frequent or constant intoxication that makes them unable to carry out even the simplest functions of living. In time, the alcoholic/addict has absolutely no ability to stop using—unless he or she enters recovery.

However, it can take a long time before those around the alcoholic/addict recognize the addiction. You should know the telltale signs of addiction before the person's life has become a complete disaster.

[Sure Signs You Can Use: AA Questionnaire]

One authoritative set of warning signs is a questionnaire prepared by Alcoholics Anonymous (familiarly termed AA). AA is a unique organization that serves as one of the most important ways to recover from alcoholism/addiction. These signs from AA represent objective guidelines with which you might gauge whether the worrisome person close to you has developed an addiction.

Answer the AA questions as impartially and honestly as you can. Ignore excuses and qualifications. Answers that start "Yes, but . . ." are not allowed. Just yes or no.

A blackout, incidentally, is a period of time when your possible alcoholic/addict was high but that, when sober the next morning or day, he or she can't recall. "But don't you remember?" you may well have said to her or him on such occasions. The addict can't recall events or conversations that occurred during the blackout periods.

• *Possible Shocks in Store*

Individuals with alcoholism often get a shock after answering these questions. (That is, if they've been able to answer them honestly. Some addicts just can't do it.) You may get the same kind of shock.

Those soon-to-be-shocked alcoholics often feel relieved to see that they answered yes to only some six or seven of the questions. Without a perfect score of twelve, they assume they have no problem and can go right on drinking.

However, the AA pamphlet identifies the number of yes answers that spell what it very conservatively calls "trouble with alcohol."

12 Test Questions from AA

Here are the AA questions. The *you* in the questions is the possible alcoholic/addict, rather than yourself. So try to answer them keeping in mind what you know about the person who is worrying you.

1. Have you ever decided to stop drinking for a week or so, but only lasted for a couple of days?
2. Do you wish people would mind their own business about your drinking—stop telling you what to do?
3. Have you ever switched from one kind of drink to another in the hope that this would keep you from getting drunk?
4. Have you had to have an eye-opener upon awakening during the past year?
5. Do you envy people who can drink without getting into trouble?
6. Have you had problems connected with drinking during the past year?
7. Has your drinking caused trouble at home?
8. Do you ever try to get "extra" drinks at a party because you do not get enough?
9. Do you tell yourself you can stop drinking any time you want to, even though you keep getting drunk when you don't mean to?

(continues)

10. Have you missed days of work or school because of drinking?
11. Do you have "blackouts"?
12. Have you ever felt that your life would be better if you did not drink?[5]

That number is a mere *four* yes answers. Four yes answers, and you're probably an alcoholic.

AA's pamphlet also observes that "only *you* [the possible alcoholic] can decide whether you think AA is for you." However, AA members also say, "If it quacks like a duck, and it walks like a duck, it probably *is* a duck."

[Symptoms List Used by Doctors]

A second set of outside guidelines you can apply to a possible alcoholic/addict who concerns you is a diagnostic test used by M.D.s—that is, by physicians, and especially physicians who are psychiatrists. These guidelines have been developed for diagnosing "substance dependence," which is the current term in professional medicine for alcoholism/addiction.

• Seven Key Symptoms
These guidelines define the prime symptoms doctors associate with alcoholism/addiction. As you'll see, they're symptoms you could identify without any special medical tests. They are the symptoms

set forth authoritatively in the *Diagnostic and Statistical Manual of Mental Disorders, Fourth Edition* (published by the American Psychiatric Association in 1994), widely termed *DSM-IV.* It gives "the official definitions for the mental disorders as these are recognized currently by clinicians from around the world." That quotation and the following passage describing the symptoms given in the *DSM-IV* for diagnosing substance dependence are reprinted by permission from a book that summarizes the *DSM-IV* information for lay readers. Its authors are the chairman of the *DSM-IV* task force and the manual's editor.

Here are those guidelines from the medical profession.

According to the diagnostic manual, you have substance dependence if:

You have developed a pattern of tolerance, withdrawal, and/or problems controlling substance use, as manifested by three or more of the following:

TOLERANCE

1. You need much more of the substance to get high than you did when you first started using it.

WITHDRAWAL

2. You get sick when you cut down or stop using the substance.

EVIDENCE OF PSYCHOLOGICAL DEPENDENCE

3. You often drink more or use more drugs than you intended.
4. You want to cut down your substance use but you can't.
5. You spend a great deal of time making sure you have the substance, using it, or getting over its effects.
6. You have given up many important social, occupational, or recreational activities because of substance use.

7. You continue to use the substance despite the fact that it has caused you physical or psychological problems (e.g., continuing to drink despite having liver problems).[6]

As with the AA questionnaire, this set of seven symptoms applies to the possible alcoholic/addict. However, it should be fairly easy for you to see if the possible alcoholic/addict in your life exhibits these symptoms, if you know that person well enough. Note that giving yes answers to only *three* of the seven symptoms spells addiction.

• *Not Necessarily Bad News*
Try not to feel downcast if your results do signify alcoholism/addiction in the person you're concerned about. Falling deeper into addiction without recognizing it makes for baffled and agonized lives for the addict and everyone around him or her. Unmasking alcoholism/addiction is the essential first step to recovery and can point the way to a far better life for all concerned.

[*One*]

The AA Way: Carrying the Message
(After Having Invented It)

Alcoholics Anonymous—*widely* termed simply AA—is the most widely available means for helping someone to recover from alcoholism/addiction. It is also very economical—it costs nothing. You'll find in AA people who know a great deal about addiction and how to get (and stay) clean and sober. These are also people who stand ready to help others start recovery and stay in it.

[How AA Can Help]

Each year, many thousands of women and men who have become addicted to alcohol and drugs start in recovery through AA. They're in all parts of the United States, and in many foreign countries. Those continuing in recovery as AA members now number some two million, according to AA reports at the time of this writing (May 2000).[1]

(Statistics about AA are approximate and estimated for reasons explained later. That they are approximations should be unimportant to you. The main point is this: Since AA helps millions of alcoholics/addicts start and stay in recovery, there's a good chance it may likewise help the person who is worrying you.)

If AA is effective for your alcoholic/addict, you'd of course feel very relieved. You would both be very fortunate. Aside from his or her recovery, though, AA can help you learn the truth about addiction.

As important, the companion (but separate) organization Al-Anon, which is described thoroughly in chapter 3, could help *you* recover from the ravages of your involvement with the alcoholic/addict. And you could thus be helped to recover whether or not the alcoholic/addict does.

Finding AA, Especially for a Crisis— Anywhere; Everywhere

You need only look in your local phone directory to reach AA throughout the United States. You'll find *AA* or *Alcoholics Anonymous* listed in the business section of the directory's white pages. An AA phone number may also be listed in the directory's yellow pages (classified phone directory listings), under a heading like "Alcoholism Information and Treatment Centers."

Outside the United States, try local phone directories or use the telephone numbers, mailing addresses, or World Wide Web home pages or e-mail addresses given in the "Sources of Help and Information" section of this book. (Of course, if you're in the United States, you can also use these additional phone numbers or addresses.)

Local police also often could tell you where and when nearby AA meetings are held.

• AA in Your Neighborhood

Very likely, groups of AA members are ready to help right in your locale. AA is a huge nonprofit society with chapters (called "groups") almost everywhere in the country. Some sixty thousand AA groups operate throughout the United States and Canada, as do forty thousand more groups in other countries around the world.[2]

It may surprise you to find AA groups nearby. AA's carefully observed principle of anonymity keeps it far more obscure than its size and importance would otherwise suggest. AA almost never advertises or publicizes.

• Denial

In all likelihood, you'd start to seek out AA in the midst of some crisis caused by the alcoholic/addict about whom you're worried. If so, you'd have been kept from calling before by denial. Unbelievably strong denial about the addiction is universally suffered by alcoholics/addicts and those involved with them. (It is also very familiar to AA members, who circulate the ironic saying, "Denial is not a river in Egypt.") Denial is also no joke. It stands as the major roadblock to breaking free of addiction. If not overcome, denial can and does kill.

Try out your local AA phone number in advance—even if you think you might not really need it. Should you face a crisis, you'd find it helpful to have the number right at hand.

• AA in a Crisis

Suppose that you phoned your local AA number during a crisis. Perhaps your alcoholic/addict was in a drunken or drugged stupor— or had just had a car accident, or had smashed the furniture, or had stormed out in the night to get more liquor or crack cocaine. What would AA do?

In a best case, a volunteer would answer your phone call. This AA member would tell you how to get immediate police or medical help, should your emergency require it. If it's not that kind of emergency, the person would give you the time and place of one or two nearby AA meetings for your alcoholic/addict to attend that day or night. In addition, you might be told that an AA member will phone you soon, if you wish, to offer to talk with your alcoholic/addict and offer to take him or her to an AA meeting.

AA custom calls for the person who offers to meet with a prospective new member to be of the same sex as the prospect (in line with a time-honored AA admonition, "men with the men, women with the women"). This is done to avoid any romantic or sexual distractions that intoxicated prospects are especially likely to seize on. Custom also dictates having two members go out on such missions, and having those members be long-experienced and fully active in the AA program. Such missions with a potential new member are termed "12th-Step calls."

Sometimes when you phone a local AA number, you'll reach an answering-machine message that may offer to have a volunteer call you later with information and help if you leave your number. The message may also tell you where else to phone for immediate aid if you need it.

• Get Medical Help

Alcohol and drugs are toxins—poisons—that damage the body in many ways, especially when abused by addicts. If the alcoholic/addict who concerns you has reached late-stage addiction, she or he needs drugs or liquor simply to push away the tortures of withdrawal.

Such withdrawal sometimes starts with violent physical reactions if she or he tries to go without the alcohol or drugs for even as little as thirty minutes. The addict needs alcohol or drugs to keep from shaking and aching all over unbearably, being racked by fevers and chills and hideous nausea, feeling a nameless, enormous dread, and even experiencing horrifying hallucinations.

Withdrawal reactions can be so intense that they kill an alcoholic. Perhaps the most frequent way in which alcohol withdrawal causes death is from convulsions or nausea. With these, the alcoholics suffocate after partially swallowing their own tongue, or choke to death on their vomit.

In order to get through such withdrawal safely and with the least distress, alcoholics/addicts who have severe addictions need to enter a medically supervised process called *detoxification*. Detox treatment usually involves being in a hospital for three to seven days. During this time, the patient's condition is carefully monitored and medicines and nutriments are given that counter withdrawal reactions.

• Finding Detox Treatment

If he or she has entered late-stage addiction, your alcoholic/addict would first need detoxification treatment before starting AA or another addiction-recovery program. AA members should be able to help you get your alcoholic/addict into a detox. (AA members know local detoxes well; some have been there, and many have helped prospects enter them.) So common is alcoholism/addiction that detox facilities are found in most hospitals today. How to find a detox and other help aside from AA is explained in chapter 2, which also tells more about the detoxing process.

Some drugs, such as marijuana and cocaine, cause less physical withdrawal torment when discontinued by an addict. However, detoxification for drugs such as these can be important to counter intense craving and emotional distress due to withdrawal.

Moreover, alcoholics/addicts who need detoxification these days most commonly have been abusing a variety of drugs and alcohol together. Some recovered addicts tell how their drugs of choice reinforced each other. One says, for instance, that cocaine enabled him to go on drinking liquor without passing out, while liquor then slowed down the frenzy of a cocaine hit so that he could go on with more cocaine a bit later—and so on.

Some alcoholics/addicts who very luckily start recovery in earlier stages can undergo withdrawal free of severe physical distress. If this is true of the one you're concerned about, recovery can start with immediate daily attendance at AA meetings without the need for initial detox.

Even someone who is starting recovery without needing detox should get an overall medical checkup. Active alcoholics/addicts typically harm their health and physical condition by abuse and neglect. Infections, malnutrition, and exhaustion often need to be cleared up. Moreover, specific and severe damage to vital organs that include the liver, heart, brain, stomach, esophagus, and pancreas due to the direct action of excessive alcohol and drugs may require treatment.

[Essential Truths You Could Learn through AA]

○ *Go to "Open" AA Meetings*

When you're inquiring or being told about AA meetings nearby, you might ask especially about "Open" Meetings. Open Meetings are ones that nonalcoholics are permitted to attend. Most AA meetings are "closed" ones—for alcoholics/addicts only. Closed meetings are held mainly to protect the anonymity of members. Membership requirements are uniquely simple, and the individual—not AA—decides whether or not the individual is a member. AA's third "tradition" (a kind of constitutional provision) states: "The only requirement for membership is a desire to stop drinking."

Notice that being a member calls merely for "a desire" to stop drinking. Some who come in find that they can't stop drinking or drugging even though they want to do so. In many cases, though, members like these eventually do stop if they keep trying to get sober and keep going to AA meetings.

By going to Open AA Meetings, you can learn essential, literally life-saving truths about alcoholism/addiction and recovery. You'd learn these most vividly from AA members talking at the meetings. You'd also learn them from AA books and pamphlets available at the meetings.

• *Have Your Alcoholic/Addict Go to AA*

Should you try to have your alcoholic/addict go along with you to the Open Meetings? Only in either of two cases: First, if doing so is the only way he or she will consider joining AA—or at least finding out about it. Or second, only if doing so reinforces his or her participation without you in closed meetings. (AAers generally recommend that new members go to a meeting every day at the start, if at all possible.) But you can go to Open Meetings whether or not your alcoholic/addict does—and, because of denial, he or she may absolutely refuse to attend, at first.

Most (though not all) AA meetings are held in the early evenings, starting right after dinnertime at an hour like 7:00, 8:00, or 8:30. Meetings typically last one hour. Such timing is common for several vital reasons. That time of day is when many alcoholics/addicts most often started drinking or drugging. It comes after the day's work. It gives the recoverer a tremendously important goal that many feel (and find) they can attain: Don't have a drink or a drug just that day—hold on until the meeting tonight. However, a great many AA meetings are also held at all hours throughout the day, particularly in larger urban areas.

[What Makes an Alcoholic/Addict Start Recovery?]

• *Hitting Bottom*

Among the essential truths about alcoholism/addiction and recovery you'd learn through AA, the most important to you is discovering what could make your alcoholic/addict start recovery. AA began in 1935 with the discovery of what can begin recovery by its two founders and their fellow early members. Subsequent experience of the members who followed, now numbering in the millions, has confirmed this discovery in virtually every individual case.

What is it? What finally breaks the iron grip of addiction and opens the way to recovery? Absolute despair. Utter hopelessness. In what has become common and widespread AA parlance, "hitting bottom."

To the alcoholic/addict—and to those who care about him or her, like you—this is terribly grim news. But the consequences from continued addiction are even grimmer. No wonder denial grows so strong.

It's the hideous nature of physical addiction that the future alcoholic/addict feels great with alcohol or drugs at the start— especially with relatively large amounts. As time goes on, larger amounts are needed more frequently in order to feel great, but even that euphoria disappears. Instead, increasing consumption is needed merely to feel normal. Then, without even more, feelings become unbearable. It's only a little less unbearable with *even more*. Full-blown addiction has set in.

• *Where Does Full-Blown Addiction Lead?*

At this point, the alcoholic/addict absolutely must sacrifice anything and everything in order to get and ingest alcohol or drugs. Inside, he or she feels terrified and borderline suicidial. Unless the drug or alcohol abuse is stopped, in time the addict may become abandoned by everyone, homeless, destitute, unemployable, ill, injured, jailed, or committed as insane. Death is not uncommon.

This is essentially what was discovered by those who started AA, and the phenomenon was described in their seminal, anonymous book, *Alcoholics Anonymous* (which first appeared in 1939, and gave the organization its name).

Controlling addiction is thus a matter of life and death. Hitting bottom is often the only thing that can stop the horrifying course of alcoholism/addiction. Hitting bottom is a time of mortal terror for the alcoholic/addict, a time when she or he can see—or is made to see—the addiction for what it is. The addict faces all the ruin and catastrophe the addiction has already wreaked, and even much worse ahead. Yet every cell in his or her body is screaming for alcohol and/or drugs.

Hitting bottom thereby makes it possible for the alcoholic/addict to accept help and to get just a glimmer of the realization that for him or her, alcohol and /or drugs might be ruinous and deadly. In rather rare cases, the alcoholic/addict has such an awakening alone. More often, it takes outsiders, like you or AA members, or health-care professionals, to help the alcoholic/addict hit bottom and start recovery.

• Catastrophe May Trigger Hitting Bottom

In quite a few cases, some shocking catastrophe brings on a "bottom." The wife or husband leaves with the kids, or threatens to do so. The car hits a telephone pole or injures a toddler. The boss finally fires the alcoholic/addict. He or she is thrown in jail for fighting in a bar, drunk driving, or drug possession. The doctor gives her or him six months to live (unless all alcohol intake stops immediately) after discovering an alcohol-damaged liver.

• The Addiction's Infinite Cruelty Can Postpone Hitting Bottom

In many cases, addiction exhibits infinite cruelty in playing with the alcoholic/addict. It can be much like a cat playing with a mouse, which cannot escape being slowly terrorized, maimed, and killed. Like the mouse that thinks this time it will run away, the alcoholic/addict may stop for a day, a week, even one or two years. But then the alcoholic/addict irresistibly goes back, in a short time worse than before.

Other expedients are endless, and always fail. He or she switches types of drinks or drugs. Too many car accidents happen, so he quits—quits driving, that is. Or she blames the locale, and moves across the country or halfway around the world. So common is this last "solution" that it's gotten a widespread name in AA, a "geographic"—that is, a futile geographic cure.

Sadly, such tortuous measures can be tried for years, while agony and loss go on and on; they may postpone hitting bottom indefinitely.

[Is AA Only for Alcoholics—Not Drug Addicts?]

• *Your Addict Is Eligible*

One objection the addict may raise is that her or his problem isn't alcohol—it's drugs. And after all, isn't this outfit *Alcoholics* Anonymous?

In reply, inform your addict that many AA groups today welcome persons with all varieties of substance-addiction problems. This is particularly true of AA groups in cities. Most recovering drug addicts today also abused alcohol as well as different drugs. Some rare AA members today abused only marijuana, or only crack cocaine, or only prescription drugs. But these new members are often welcomed all the same by their AA groups.

If your addict should encounter an AA group that seems a bit unfriendly, he or she could find and join another group whose members include some successfully recovering drug addicts. Many groups share a view commonly expressed at AA meetings: "A drug is a drug"—whether it's alcohol or cocaine, heroin or marijuana, Percodan or Valium, or whatever. Moreover, by basic principle, no AA group can exclude anyone who wants to join and states that he or she "has a desire to stop drinking"—AA's only membership requirement.

• *Narcotics Anonymous (NA) and Cocaine Anonymous (CA)*

Two organizations similar to AA were organized for drug addicts in past years. One of these may appeal to your drug addict instead of AA. Narcotics Anonymous, or NA, and Cocaine Anonymous, or CA. NA and CA came into existence when a number of addicts found that AA's method and principles seemed to prove about as effective for drug addiction as for alcoholism. However, in those years several decades ago, many AA leaders and groups resisted opening AA to persons who were mainly drug addicts. These leaders feared that AA's proven value against alcoholism might be fatally compromised if AA should lose credibility by trying to counter drug addiction and failing. Some were concerned about the illegality of drugs.

Curiously, then, as a result, NA and CA were organized with exactly the same approach as AA. Even the same AA words were used for the basic "12 Steps" of NA and CA, with only the words *narcotics* and *cocaine* substituted for *alcohol.*

Compared to the number of AA groups, fewer NA and CA groups function today. Some NA or CA members prefer them to AA groups, feeling that the struggles of fellow addicts most closely parallel their own experience and thus better help bolster their recovery. If the alcoholic/addict in your life may be interested, you can find out how to get in touch with NA or CA and their groups in the "Sources of Help and Information" section at the end of this book.

You may find it helpful to know that AA's methods and principles have also been applied in still other "anonymous" societies dealing with habit-forming problem behaviors. Perhaps the two largest of these are OA (Overeaters Anonymous) and GA (Gamblers Anonymous).

Neither the official AA central organization nor AA groups have any connection with or any formal role in these other organizations termed "anonymous."

[Outside Experts Evaluate AA]

You may be wondering what respected authorities independent of AA conclude about the program's effectiveness. Here are two examples.

Dr. Allen Frances and Dr. Michael B. First, who were respectively the task-force chairman and the editor of *DSM-IV*—the most recent edition of the definitive professional reference work for psychiatrists—say this about AA in their "layman's guide to the psychiatrist's bible," *Your Mental Health*:

Alcoholics Anonymous (and its offshoots) is the great success story in the treatment of addictions. On any given day, more people go to AA groups around the world than attend any other form of therapy. The message of AA is compelling and translates very well across different drugs, social classes, and cultures. AA groups are so numerous and so varied that almost anyone can find a congenial one that is readily available, conveniently located, and probably meeting that night. AA provides hope, a philosophy of life, a spiritual reawakening, an emotional experience, concrete support, a sounding board, great advice, and help for family members. It is all the more remarkable that it does all this with virtually no bureaucracy or budget.[3]

A second opinion on the value of AA is expressed by another psychiatrist, Dr. George E. Vaillant. Dr. Vaillant led and wrote a report on one of the most authoritative studies ever made of alcoholism and alcoholics. This monumental research project followed and analyzed the lives of more than six hundred persons for more than forty years. Its findings were presented in Dr. Vaillant's books, *The Natural History of Alcoholism* (1983) and *The Natural History of Alcoholism Revisited* (1995). In his second book, Dr. Vaillant stated:

> More recovered alcoholics from both groups [two large groups of men studied in the research] began stable abstinence while attending Alcoholics Anonymous than while attending alcohol treatment centers.

Dr. Vaillant added that, on the basis of findings for these two groups and an additional one he had studied:

> The numbers of subjects in these studies are small, and these results, drawn primarily from middle-aged white males, must be interpreted with caution. The implication from the three samples, however, is that a great many severely alcohol-dependent Americans, regardless of their social or psychological makeup, find help for their alcoholism through Alcoholics Anonymous.[4]

[Personal Histories]

From the start, AA has relied on tremendously moving firsthand stories of individual men and women—who tell about their lives in the hope of getting other alcoholics/addicts started on recovery—rather than on statistics or research findings. As a speaker at an Open AA Meeting once put it when sharing what worked with him and what also works for others in his own twelve-step efforts: "When I say what I think, it has no power. But when I tell about my life and all that I've gone through—that has the power."

That power was one of AA's original startling discoveries. An alcoholic who is in fact recovering from alcoholism in many cases has more power than anyone else to break through to what AA calls to this day, "the still-suffering alcoholic."

The first-edition *Alcoholics Anonymous* volume of 1939 states:

Highly competent psychiatrists who have dealt with us [alcoholics] have found it sometimes impossible to persuade an alcoholic to discuss his situation without reserve. Strangely enough, wives, parents, and intimate friends usually find us even more unapproachable than do the psychiatrist and the doctor.

But the ex-problem drinker who has found this solution [AA], *who is properly armed with facts about himself, can generally win the entire confidence of another alcoholic in a few hours. Until such an understanding is reached, little or nothing can be accomplished.* [Italics in the original.][5]

- *Life Stories at the Open Meetings*

You can experience the power of life stories like these directly—in person—at the major type of AA's Open Meetings. These are informally called "speaker" meetings. At them, the frequent custom is to have from one to three speakers "tell their stories."

Time-honored advice for telling your story calls for a speaker to cover three main things:

- what it used to be like, while "active" (that is, actively drinking/drugging);
- what happened to get you into recovery and AA; and
- what it's been like in recovery.

A meeting chairperson or other meeting leader introducing the speakers is very likely to set forth two vital guidelines for the listeners. One centers on AA's principle of anonymity. It is usually phrased, "What you hear here, and who you see here, let it stay here." Anything said, and anyone seen, are not to be mentioned to anyone outside that room.

Alcoholics/addicts attending are the target of the second admonition. "Identify. Don't compare," the leader typically warns. Identify with the feelings that a speaker sets forth, a leader often goes on to explain. Don't compare the disasters and troubles of a speaker with the disasters and troubles in your active-addiction days.

By comparing that you didn't have as many car wrecks or jailings or job losses or psych wards as a speaker did, you might compare yourself right out the door and back into drinking and drugging, the leader might add. But if you instead identify with a speaker's feelings, you'll know in your bones that you often felt (and sometimes still feel) exactly the same way.

If the alcoholic/addict you wish to help would be able to identify like this at Open Meetings, she or he might be strongly reinforced to get started in recovery. Especially if she or he should happen to have that electrifying experience of needing to gasp to a speaker: "You told *my* story!" Sooner or later, if the alcoholic/addict keeps attending meetings, just that happens. Always.

[Two Unlikely Addicts]

The eloquence of even a little-schooled, rough-and-tumble speaker at an AA Open Meeting can prove surprising, and also moving. This results because speakers can talk about themselves with a rare degree of openness and trust made possible by AA's unique qualities as an organization. Also motivating the speakers are deep convictions that what they say with complete honesty mightily helps buttress their own sobriety and may even help save someone else's life. Such sharing of "experience, strength, and hope" between one alcoholic and another has represented one of AA's main curative powers from the beginning.

The following two examples may just barely suggest how some speaker at an AA Open Meeting might have a powerful effect on the alcoholic/addict in your life.

• *Oil-Rigs Roustabout from a Rich Family*
"Hi, I'm Frank. I'm an addict and alcoholic," says the powerfully built, lean young man standing at the front of the room. You're in the basement room of a church parish hall at an after-dinner hour one weekday evening. You and the very mixed assortment of some thirty or so people are sitting on metal folding chairs. Frank, the

speaker, has given the currently common opening remark whenever a member talks at a meeting (one's nickname or first name and "I'm an alcoholic" or "addict"). Two lettered signs hang on the front wall. One is headed, THE TWELVE STEPS. The other is titled: THE TWELVE TRADITIONS.

Frank relates how he grew up on the two-hundred-acre estate of his folks in the rolling hills outside Seattle. He got shipped off to private boarding school when only ten years old. He hated it at first. He soon ran across some other boys who turned him on to pot and speed. In a couple of years they added LSD to the mix. Tripping out on all this stuff was just great, he found. He found it all still more exciting when he went on to dealing in drugs himself.

Frank got caught and kicked out around age sixteen or so. At the next two boarding schools the same thing happened. Mom and Dad then shipped him off to two wilderness-survival, Outward Bound–style programs, one in the American Rockies, and the other in the Peruvian Andes. Then came a couple of very foggy college years heavily laced with alcohol and finally ending with his expulsion for again dealing drugs.

Once home, Frank took his big Harley-Davidson motorcycle out touring and wound up in the Texas oil fields. He started work there as a roustabout on the rigs drilling new wells. Even more than the very dangerous and very heavy physical labor with huge steel casings and drill bits and guide chains, he liked the company of really tough guys who drank as hard as he did starting right after every day's work. Drinking and work filled his life seven days a week. In two years in the oil fields, Frank took off only one day, a Christmas Day. Gruesome accidents on the job crippled or killed a friend now and then, but Frank kept right on working.

Finally that got too crazy, so he tried college again for a while.

By this time he couldn't stand being anywhere but alone at the far end of the bar while he drank. On campus one day, some young college punk carelessly bumped him aside to go through a door. In a lightning oil-field reaction, Frank slammed the boy against the wall but stopped just before beating him senseless. That alarmed Frank. He felt he'd turned into an animal. He left the college and biked home on the Harley.

By this time the booze and the drugs had him completely. He slaved like a dog maintaining his parents' estate, doing all the mowing, all the dangerous tree work of felling huge trees and clearing new fields and pruning dead limbs, all the painting and repairs on the outbuildings and mansion. He worked alone. Nights he went off by himself to drink at bars. Towering rages would sweep over him on his workdays outdoors, and he would smash logs and rocks.

Most of the time, though, he felt absolutely hopeless, and in a black despair. Drinking and drugs no longer brought any cheer or excitement. They merely dulled the hopelessness and pain for just a few minutes. And when he went any more than a few hours without them, the black despair dropped down to terror, and he started feeling physically sick.

One night when Frank felt especially wretched, a boyhood friend whom he used to drink with came by. The friend asked Frank to come along with him to an AA meeting. Frank has no idea why he said yes. He did go along. Frank guesses that he'd reached the point where he was sick and tired of being sick and tired, as an old AA saying goes. Or maybe some angel just smiled on him that night, he says.

Frank is one of the lucky ones for whom AA clicked almost from the start. It felt like he had come home at last. For years he'd thought that he was the only one on the planet who acted and reacted the way he did. But here was a whole roomful of people who had gone through many of the same kinds of experiences and who'd felt the same hopelessness. And from their smiles and the light in their eyes and what they said of their lives, they had found a way out. He wanted what they had.

• *How AA Members Fight Urges to Drink or to Drug*

He was amazed especially that they fought off that irresistible craving to drink and to drug. How? With various basic tools, perfected by many over the years. A prime one is that AA members don't vow to quit forever. They simply don't drink or drug today. They quit "one day at a time," as they endlessly remark. And if that gets too tough, they don't use for just one hour at a time. Or on occasion, one minute at a time. And they are given phone numbers by other men (or other women, for a woman). And if they feel an urge to use getting strong, they phone or see another member and confess the urge and get bolstered by the member not to give in because that insane urge will soon pass and be gone.

Another vital basic for him, Frank says, was the saying, "It's the first drink that gets you drunk—not the tenth or fifteenth." This is paradoxically true for anyone who has become addicted—the addict has lost the power to decide when to stop or how to act after the first drink or drug. Frank likes the time-honored comparison to getting hit by a train. "It's the locomotive that kills you," he says, "not the caboose."

At the start Frank was told that it gets better and it keeps on getting better the longer you stay with the AA program. Frank briefly sums up how he worked the Twelve Steps of the AA program with his AA sponsor as his experienced guide. Those steps especially opened up a whole new life for him, he says.

Now he has a wife he's crazy about and two darling little kids. He's gotten free of the stifling influence of his mom and dad, yet has still found how to give them his full affection. He started his own landscaping business, and it's doing very well. Thanks to the program, he says, his life has gotten better than he'd ever dreamed.

For the newcomer, he says: If it happened for me, it can happen for you. Just keep coming. Don't drink or drug, and go to meetings one day at a time, and you, too, will get a great life.

• *Regal Beauty Who Had Everything but Couldn't Stop*
"Hi. I'm Elaine, and I'm an alcoholic." The speaker at this AA meeting has a really striking appearance, you think. She's tall, trim, blond, blue-eyed, tanned, and chic in a simple, sleeveless black tube dress.

She grew up in Winnetka, a fashionable suburb on Lake Michigan, north of Chicago, where her dad was a very successful lawyer, she says. Their lives were extremely comfortable. Tutors, summer trips to Europe, country club parties and sports, expensive cars, a splendid house right on the lake.

Her mom and dad drank, of course. Everyone did. For her parents, it was one of the social graces, part of good living. On holidays, many weekends, and special occasions, cocktails before dinner, vintage wines with dinner, and fine liqueurs and cordials after dinner.

Mom and Dad let Elaine have occasional sips of one of the sweet wines like port or sherry as an older child. In her teens, they carefully introduced her to proper drinking, "drinking like a lady," when she began going out to dances and parties on dates. Elaine hadn't yet reached legal drinking age, but no one in their set paid any attention to that—except not to get caught. Mom and Dad did warn and guard her against taking any chances with drunk drivers.

Elaine fell deeply in love with one endearing boy in her late teens, even though on occasion he'd get terribly drunk. And one day she was heartbroken to hear that, driving home late the night before, he'd killed himself skidding off a curve and hitting a tree. She says that that may have had much to do with her deciding while in college to become a certified alcoholism counselor, a CAC.

Shaking her head, Elaine says it's unbelievable how she never saw her drinking start to be a problem. She went on after college to marry a corporation lawyer, have two children, and go back into her counseling work when the kids were in high school. Their life was much the same as her life had been while growing up—gracious good living, with no money problems at all.

George, her husband, worked hard and, on occasion, drank hard. Elaine had no trouble keeping up with his drinking. In fact, at parties when he was starting to slur his speech and sway on his feet, Elaine would still be steady as a rock and would drive them home.

Her drinking began to change so gradually that it was only by looking back that she could glimpse what had happened, Elaine says. First it was having another highball or two once George had been tucked into bed after she'd driven them home. Then it was downing cocktails—"just one or two," she recalls having told her-self—in the kitchen while getting dinner when George was away on one of his many business trips.

One evening at dinner, George joked that he liked her new habit of fixing them cocktails every night without fail. But, he went on, what might her counseling clients think of her possibly heading down the same road as them? He laughed loud and long at the thought.

Elaine, though, was aghast. No more drinking that anyone sees, she silently swore to herself. She went on getting George cocktails, and going out to dinners and parties with him just as before. But on all these occasions, she drank only tonics, juices, or spring waters—no alcohol. If George or anyone asked, she'd casually say she just didn't care for alcohol anymore, but certainly didn't want to spoil anyone else's enjoyment of drinking.

In time, in a slow unfolding, Elaine found her life turning ever more hard and bleak. She had so much to do, every day! Every minute, with her home, her kids, her work, their social life—it was always go, go, go! She felt she deserved some relief, had to have some relief.

Finally, one night after everyone was asleep, she got a vodka bottle from the liquor cabinet and took it into her walk-in clothes closet. Her mind was a blank. It felt like a dream, but she knew it was real.

She huddled down on the floor in a corner and drank right from the bottle. Oh, what relief! What blessed relief! She kept on drinking until she passed out. Some time before morning, she woke with a sharp stab of terror of being found out. She soundlessly put the bottle back, and climbed into bed.

Through the following weeks, her need for these closet binges came over her more often. In time, it was every night. Some mornings, she vowed she would stop, but by night never could.

In some part of her mind, she sensed where she was headed. But that made her only more desperate during her high-pressured daytime hours. She took on ever more responsibilities and tasks to prove there was nothing wrong.

Elaine felt especially torn to be working with clients who were struggling as hard as they could not to take any alcohol or drugs at all. But she tried to brush that aside by telling herself they were much worse than she was—that she really didn't have a problem because she knew so much, and she worked so hard and so well.

Then, one horrifying night, the closet door opened and there stood George. Elaine never asked how he happened to be there. She had burst into tears and sobbed that she needed help.

She would be eternally grateful that George understood, she says. Right away, she went off to a four-week inpatient rehabilitation program that started with several days' detox. Elaine had felt utterly crushed on arriving, utterly beaten and hopeless. She couldn't choke back her tears in the middle of the admitting-office questions. But then the older staff member who was asking the questions had gotten up, come over, and given Elaine a hug.

Elaine will never forget how the woman had told her, "It's over, dear. It's really over."

Elaine had been so deeply shaken by her bottom that she started going to AA meetings every night as soon as she left the rehab. Today, Elaine says, her life is outwardly much the same as before—her home life with George and the children, her work, their friends and social life. Inwardly, though, it all seems completely different. An old, nagging, deep-seated inadequacy is gone. Her compulsion to drink was lifted early, while still in rehab. Brief thoughts of drinking are rare. She ends them right away by phoning or seeing her AA sponsor or another AA friend.

Elaine now has, she says, "an abiding peace of mind" that has transformed everything in her life. "But, most important," she says, "if you're like I was when I started, you have no hope at all that anything can help. For me, I knew so much about this disease that I was certain nothing could save me. Nothing. I was terrified. Totally without hope. If you're like that right now, take heart. This program really did work for me. And it really can work for you, too."

> ## What AA Basics Would Your Alcoholic/Addict Follow to Recover?

Simplicity is a prime virtue of AA's program for surviving the ruinous and often fatal disease of alcoholism/addiction. Everything in AA aims at one supreme, single point: Don't drink or drug. Not in even the slightest quantity. Not for any reason, no matter what happens. Not at any moment.

In essence, this is the only fundamental element of AA that's absolutely necessary for recovery by the alcoholic/addict you're concerned about. Notoriously, though, one of the main definitions of an alcoholic/addict is someone who cannot possibly stop.

• *One Day at a Time, Don't Drink or Drug—and Go to a Meeting*

So, AA members ask the newcomer, can you stop just for one day—*this* day, now? The newcomer who doesn't need detox badly enough, and who is already hitting bottom badly enough, will say yes.

Fine, say AA members. We just don't drink or drug "one day at a time." *This* day. Today. And we get to an AA meeting tonight. Every night, at first.

At the meeting, members say, you'll find that we're all kinds of people who know all about how to stay away from a drink or a drug one day at a time. We will welcome you, and we'll offer to help you by really caring about you—the way others cared about us when we were new. You'll learn from us how we've gone through all that you've gone through. (Some of us have gone through even more.) You'll learn what we do so that we still don't have to drink or drug.

And, with us, they say, you'll find that you don't have to drink or drug today, either. If you do what we do, you'll get what we've got: a life, a life clean and sober, a good life, in recovery.

• AA Members Help Your Alcoholic/Addict, and Their Own Recovery

Passages earlier in the chapter told about AA's discovery of the unique power often possessed by a recovering alcoholic/addict to get an active alcoholic/addict started on recovery. AA made an even more important companion discovery concerning such power. This power works both ways—it works on the alcoholic/addict trying to help, as much as on the alcoholic/addict needing help. In fact, it typically proves more consistently effective on the helper than on the one being helped.

Discovery of this reverse effect on the helper marked the founding of AA. Future founder Bill W. discovered that he could not preserve his own then-new and shaky sobriety alone, by his own efforts. He could save his sobriety, his freedom from addiction, only by trying to help a hopelessly addicted and alcoholic Akron physician, Dr. Bob S., to start on recovery.

Bill did try (essentially by telling Dr. Bob his story), and stayed sober himself. The date of Dr. Bob's last drink, on June 10, 1935, is AA's founding date. Dr. Bob is the other founder. Each of the two drunks helping the other stayed sober. Alone, neither could do it.

• *"Passing It On"*

Ever since then, every AA member gratefully recalls getting extraordinary help when new to the program from longer-experienced members who said that any all-out help they gave greatly protected their own sobriety. They were passing it on, giving to others what had been given to them.

Helping others to recover as the best protection of one's own recovery thus became one of the most effective parts of the "message" invented by AA—the message that here at last in human history is a way by which a great many previously hopeless alcoholics/addicts actually are recovering. AA members today accordingly try to "carry this message to alcoholics," as it says in AA's Twelfth Step.

• *"You Can't Do It Alone—and You Don't Have To"*

In almost anything he or she does in AA, the alcoholic/addict you care about will be helped by members carrying the message to him or her with their actions and words. In turn, your alcoholic/addict is likely to start helping in simple ways, such as going to and honestly speaking up in meetings, talking with others before and after meetings, setting up and putting away meeting chairs, and phoning other men (for a man) or women (for a woman) who are members. Getting involved with others in ways like these has been found extremely important to promoting recovery.

"It's a *we* program," members often observe. "I drank and drugged alone, but we get sober together."

"You can't do this thing alone," one member recalls having been told in his early days. He was immensely heartened to hear what followed: "And you don't have to."

• *Join an AA Group Soon*

Two more basic commitments will almost certainly be "suggested" to the alcoholic/addict when he or she starts going to AA meetings. These are to join an AA group and to get an AA sponsor—and to do both in one's first few meetings.

Incidentally, AA members merely "suggest" by tradition, in order to avoid alienating the often rebellious newcomer. Members typically accompany a suggestion by describing how they had felt much like the newcomer does at the moment, and how acting on the suggestion had eased their difficulty.

Joining a group is usually very simple, and is generally done by just giving a group meeting leader or chairperson one's name, phone number, and date of last drink or drug. As noted earlier, anyone who says that she or he has "a desire to stop drinking" meets all the requirements for joining any AA group. Only the individual need make that decision to join. No AA group can reject his or her membership.

Often it helps to choose a group that has meetings that occur at the most convenient places and times. Newcomers sometimes sample a few different groups in order to see which one might feel most congenial. More important than sampling, though, is joining soon. Drifting among groups can be a kind of drifting away. Besides, members are free to change groups anytime later if they want.

• *Get a Sponsor Soon*

Choosing a "sponsor" as soon as possible in the group that one joins is also suggested to a newcomer.

A sponsor for something like a country club or fraternal order is someone who proposes one for membership. However, an AA sponsor is different. A sponsor usually has at least a year's sober experience in AA and serves as a guide to the AA program. Most often, it's thought that the sponsor should be of the same sex as the person sponsored (again, to avoid risking any possible romantic distraction from the vital task of staying sober).

In many groups, it's customary for the newcomer to ask an experienced member to be his or her sponsor. It's suggested that the member asked be a person whose sobriety and grasp of the AA program seem especially strong from what the newcomer can gather in one or a few early meetings. Some groups have a "temporary sponsor" list of members who have volunteered to serve in that capacity. A newcomer may be given a temporary sponsor from such a list.

Good reasons stand behind suggestions to get a sponsor no later than one's first few meetings. Wide experience has shown personal guidance from a sponsor to be especially helpful when starting out in AA. And one can change to another sponsor at any time for whatever reason. On the other hand, some initial sponsors continue with the people they sponsor for many years.

• *Basic Actions Enable Your Alcoholic/Addict to Learn More*

If the alcoholic/addict gets through these basic actions, she or he has a very good chance of staying in recovery. He or she will learn a great deal more, especially about his or her own character and past, and about tailoring AA's powerful and very many resources to his or her individual needs for safeguarding recovery. He or she will learn most vitally through other members. Reading AA books, pamphlets, and articles would also help.

Depending on how close you are, the alcoholic/addict starting in recovery may share with you something of all that's being learned. You could also get the gist of much of it by continuing to go to

AA Open Meetings. You'd find it informative, too, to read AA literature, especially a current edition of *Alcoholics Anonymous* (traditionally called "the big book" in AA).

You yourself could safely afford to rely on reading for almost all of what you might want to know about AA. However, the alcoholic/addict in your life could do so only at risk. Exhaustive painful experience has shown that one cannot read oneself into recovery. One has to live it, with like souls.

• AA's Unique Character Fosters Recovery

You and the alcoholic/addict would find AA unlike any other organization you've ever known. Its unique anonymity means that members generally avoid incurring public scorn as despicable drunks and addicts (even though recovering).

Anonymity in addition cultivates an atmosphere in meetings where members can be as completely honest about their addiction-caused wrongdoings and failures and scandals as they wish, and not be judged or gossiped about but instead be understood as having developed the disease of addiction—and be thus understood because everyone else there needs to be freed of just such shame and guilt. Honesty—especially about ever-recurring urges to drink and to drug, and about troubles that can bring urges on—helps break addiction's denial.

AA is by basic provision exclusively self-supporting and absolutely nonprofit. Passing the basket at meetings (and having members who can afford it toss in a dollar) is the very widespread way in which groups pay for meeting places and refreshments. No one in any group gets paid for anything he or she does in AA. There is no money whatever to be made in AA. This keeps newcomers like your alcoholic/addict from suspecting he or she is being exploited for money.

Your alcoholic/addict should find no one on power trips in any AA group. AA's Tradition Twelve decrees, in part, "place principles before personalities." By custom, all group office holders—group chairpersons and steering committee members, and meeting chairpersons—rotate out of office every few months.

Paperwork and records are virtually nonexistent in AA groups, so that as much of the volunteer members' time as possible will go into helping newcomers and troubled members get and stay sober. Also, group membership records are kept to the barest minimum (almost always, with no last names) and are kept strictly confidential in order to protect AA's supreme anonymity principle. As a result, statistics about AA's effectiveness and even its total membership are approximations based on surveys, sampling, and special studies.

• AA's Effectiveness and Size

AA does have a General Service Office (GSO) in New York City at which some 110 full-time employees handle the production and distribution of official AA books and pamphlets. (These are sold essentially at cost, and almost exclusively to AA groups.) GSO employees also edit and issue AA's monthly magazine, the *A.A. Grapevine*. They carry out the tasks of liaison and communication assigned GSO by AA's extensive and active, all-volunteer structure of representation linking individual groups through district and area bodies to a central General Service Conference of delegates representing areas. This conference and the GSO technically serve the United States and Canada, but they also cooperate with and help out AA groups and bodies in many other countries.

Based on its latest triennial survey (made in 1998), GSO reported that AA had approximately two million current members worldwide, with some hundred thousand AA groups. Those groups functioned in more than one hundred countries.

Moreover, the GSO survey indicated that, among all AA members, 47 percent had been sober more than five years, 26 percent had been sober for one to five years, and 27 percent had been sober for less than one year.

• *Alternatives to AA*

One other characteristic of AA is its typical open-mindedness regarding any other source of help with recovery from alcoholism/addiction. The AA way may not prove to be effective just by itself, or may not be acceptable at all, to some alcoholics/addicts. This might turn out to be the case with the alcoholic/addict you're concerned about. If so, you have every reason to keep up your hopes. For such alcoholics/addicts, AA members will often urge other sources of help. Quite often, these are professional sources like those described in the next chapter.

[*Two*]

The Professional Way: Intervention, Detox, Rehab, Aftercare

rofessionals in the treatment of alcoholism/addiction could
prove to be especially powerful allies in your efforts to help the
alcoholic/addict. By principle, AA and its members do not provide
any medical or therapeutic professional services, which can be very
important to the recovery (and even the survival) of alcoholics/addicts. AA's eighth "tradition" (or basic principle) states that "Alcoholics Anonymous should remain forever nonprofessional." AA
members accordingly value and, as needed, draw on such vital services by seeking help from professionals outside the group.

[A Crisis May Trigger Getting Professional Help]

There's some chance that a crisis may force you to turn to professionals for help with an alcoholic/addict. One such crisis could involve violence or injury caused by the alcoholic/addict.

Intoxicated alcoholics/addicts often injure themselves or others
and commit reckless, dangerous acts. Some hooked on drugs may

overdose and lapse into a coma. Late-stage alcoholics can go into convulsions or get heart attacks. The loved ones of addicts must be ready to immediately phone for the police at any time (by dialing 911, in much of the United States) or to get hospital emergency services.

• *Seeking Help for an Addiction Distress Crisis*

In another common crisis afflicting persons in the late stages of alcoholism/addiction, the individual becomes so physically sickened and crazed that he or she badly needs medical help. The person then asks for—or at least doesn't resist—seeing a doctor. The help he or she needs at times like these is a type of medical treatment called detoxification. As the name suggests, such treatment is needed to counteract the poisonous effects of all the alcohol or drugs the person has taken.

• *Finding Detox Facilities in Advance*

Again, if you live with an alcoholic/addict, it's wise for you to locate in advance detoxification services that may be needed in an emergency. One way to find out about these would be to ask AA members, if you've been going to Open AA Meetings. Or, if you've started going to Al-Anon meetings (as suggested in chapter 3), you could ask fellow Al-Anon members.

Either AA or Al-Anon members should be able to tell you about such detox facilities in the area. Some of those in AA might also be willing to help take your alcoholic/addict to be detoxified when the need arises. In addition, volunteers at the AA information phone number given in your local telephone directory (as explained in chapter 1) should be able to tell you where to find nearby detoxes.

Another way to find a facility is to look in the yellow pages of a local classified telephone directory. First, find such category listings as: "Alcoholism Information and Treatment Centers" or "Drug Abuse and Addiction—Information and Treatment."

Within such categories, you'll see listings of organizations or hospitals that provide detoxification. You might phone two or three possibilities for important details such as types of alcoholics/addicts they detox, hours of admission, costs, and whether their program is licensed by the state.

• *Rush to a Hospital Emergency Room*

If you are unable to locate a detox facility in this way, take your alcoholic/addict to the nearest hospital emergency room. If an emergency arises, move quickly. Seek help immediately for your alcoholic/addict at a detox facility or the closest emergency room.

Most important to you before an emergency, though, is the following professional method you could initiate in an effort to start your alcoholic/addict into recovery early, before some highly damaging crises occur.

Mounting an "Intervention"

One possibly beneficial option open to you before a serious crisis happens is getting a professional to plan and coordinate a special method for starting your alcoholic/addict in recovery. The major professional method for doing this is called an intervention.

Dissatisfaction with the general view in AA that recovery could start only after the alcoholic had "hit bottom" led to the development of this intervention method. It was pioneered by Vernon E. Johnson, a Doctor of Divinity and counselor. Dr. Johnson made a study of some two hundred alcoholics in the 1960s. In part, it sought to determine what had caused the alcoholics to begin recovery. The main answer: crises. Crises so bad and with enough impact that the alcoholics had been shocked into getting help with ending the enormous havoc wreaked by their addiction.

This discovery led to the idea that the most significant people in the alcoholic's life might not need to wait through perhaps years of ever-worsening agony and loss. Instead, those people might be able to stage a crisis that breaks through the alcoholic's denial. They could *intervene*. Over the years, Dr. Johnson and his associates at the Johnson Institute in Minneapolis, Minnesota, introduced and developed techniques by which just such a decisive crisis of caring confrontation could be created.

Vernon Johnson's fervor is reflected in an opening argument in his classic work, *Intervention: How to Help Someone Who Doesn't Want Help.* In it, he decried the time-honored approach of waiting for the addict to hit bottom. You need not "stand by and watch the chemically dependent person plumb the depths of suffering and despair before doing something about it," he wrote. "You don't have to bide your time until your family breaks up, or the person is fired from his or her job—or kills someone in a car accident. You can reach out *now.*"

• *Finding a Counselor Skilled in Intervention*
Should you want to consider this option, it might be best for you to locate and talk with a counselor specializing in chemical dependency and interventions of this type. You should be able to find such specialists by telephoning several of the treatment facilities for alcoholism/addiction in your area. (You could locate these treatment facilities in the same ways described earlier for locating detox

facilities; some treatment facilities would, in fact, be the same ones that offer detox services.) When calling each treatment facility, ask if they offer professional services for coordinating such interventions for alcoholism/addiction. If they do, ask for details—especially ones concerning what those services are and how effective they have proved in their experience.

Specify in these inquiries that you mean intervention meetings of the Johnson Institute type. Why? Because the term *intervention* is widely used by treatment professionals today to refer to starting any type of treatment for alcoholism/addiction. However, in this book, intervention refers only to the Johnson Institute variety.

• *Check Out Your Intervention Counselor*

By all means make sure that the intervention counselor you choose has full professional competence. It's perfectly legitimate for you to ask a counselor whom you're seriously considering about his or her professional training, credentials, and experience in coordinating interventions.

Perhaps the most important additional qualification to seek is the counselor's dedication to avoid having the intervention emotionally demolish the alcoholic/addict so badly that subsequent treatment loses effectiveness. Try to make sure that your interventionist hates the disease rather than its victims, that, in fact, he or she cares enormously about its victims.

As an alternative to using a counselor, you could set about conducting an intervention yourself by studying the books on intervention identified in this book's "Sources of Help and Information" section. However, carrying out an intervention is a complex process that requires special skills, training, and experience for its effectiveness. Concerned nonprofessionals have carried out interventions on some occasions. But an intervention is far more likely to move the alcoholic/addict into treatment and to benefit each of the participants when guided by a professional interventionist.

• *Confronting the Alcoholic/Addict*

You'd begin learning about an intervention and how it's run shortly after starting work sessions with your chosen intervention counselor. You'd find out that, in basic outline, an intervention is a meeting in which the alcoholic/addict is typically surprised to be brought together with a planned gathering of other people. It's recommended that the intervention be sprung on the unsuspecting alcoholic/addict at a time when she or he is sober.

In the gathering are as many as possible of the people he or she most cares about and most heavily depends on. Among them are such people as: lover or spouse, employer or business partner (or most important client or customer), brothers, sisters, children, parents, grandparents, minister, priest, rabbi, closest friends, other closest relatives.

Everyone there except the alcoholic/addict has very carefully prepared and rehearsed his or her part in the intervention, which has been very elaborately and skillfully planned. Planning and organizing have been carried out by a leader of the meeting with the guidance and help of the intervention counselor. The counselor does not act as the meeting leader, but instead serves as a facilitator who helps prepare and assist with guidance in the meeting. The leader is a concerned person like yourself who volunteers for the role.

In summary, the intervention meeting opens with the leader saying essentially that everyone there cares deeply for the alcoholic/addict but is terribly worried about the effects of alcohol and/or drugs on the alcoholic/addict. The alcoholic/addict is asked simply to listen as each person speaks. He or she is asked not to respond until after all the others have spoken.

Then, each of the others in turn first tells how much they care about the alcoholic/addict. Next, the person recounts the facts of what happened, in incident after incident after incident, when the alcoholic/addict was drinking or drugging. For each incident, the person also describes their intensely painful feelings at that time— feelings like bitter disappointment, humiliation, heartbreak, shame, anger, or fear.

Often, the others will each say three things more. They will express their encouragement for the alcoholic/addict to accept immediate help. They will declare their willingness to do all they can for the alcoholic/addict if he or she gets help. But they add that they will no longer tolerate or condone any more addictive behavior.

• *Immediate Treatment*

At the end, the leader sums up that everyone there wants the alcoholic/addict to begin treatment and end all the damage and hurt. Arrangements have been made for the alcoholic/addict to start in a treatment program immediately, the leader says. Any reason for postponement involving work or family or friends or finances has already also been disposed of. Even the luggage has been packed, if live-in treatment has been set. The leader adds, please, agree to go.

If the alcoholic/addict at first says no, the leader says he or she may want to reconsider. There are consequences. Each person has decided beforehand what they will do if treatment is refused. Each in turn then reports their decision, starting with the most serious. These may include such consequences as: being fired from the job, being divorced, having to move out of the home, having the lover or spouse leave, not seeing the children.

As you might expect, carefully planned interventions usually do lead the alcoholic/addict to start in a treatment program.

• *What If the Alcoholic/Addict Won't Accept Treatment?*

In only very few cases of interventions carefully planned with the help of a skilled professional will the alcoholic/addict refuse to enter treatment regardless of consequences. You'd of course be disappointed should this happen for you. However, many positive results would have been achieved.

Denial and all its strangling web of lies and deceit would have been broken. You and all participants would then clearly see lines of positive action to take—carrying out the decisions you had outlined to the alcoholic/addict as consequences. You would have started opening a way out of a nightmare life for the alcoholic/addict. This way out is one that he or she is far more likely to take at some time sooner than would have been true before the intervention. Best of all, you and the other participants would have left your roles in that nightmare life behind, forever.

In some cases of refusal of treatment by the alcoholic/addict, still another predetermined alternative may be offered by the group of concerned persons. One alternative may be a contract to immediately enter the selected treatment program if a relapse occurs. Another alternative may be to immediately enter a less intensive treatment than the one originally selected.

[What Treatment Programs Are Available]

Authorities on intervention deem it especially important to have everything ready for a willing alcoholic/addict to start in a treatment program immediately at the end of the intervention. It's also possible that, even without a formal intervention, the alcoholic/addict you're concerned about may somehow hit bottom and ask to go into treatment. In either case, here's what you'd need to know about treatment programs and arranging for them.

• *Laws Protect Against Privacy Invasion and Criminal Prosecution*
You may be worried that by starting to talk to professionals about someone who needs treatment you might harm the alcoholic/addict you're trying to help. This possibility may also worry the alcoholic/addict. After all, mere possession of street drugs is certainly a crime. And addiction to alcohol or drugs is notoriously ruinous to job prospects, or to the reputation of anyone who's in business or a profession or even community life, if word of such addiction gets out. Of course, eminently practical reasons like these have long motivated the vital anonymity of Alcoholics Anonymous (and the various derivative twelve-step "anonymous" organizations).

You and your alcoholic/addict need not worry. Concerns like yours have been entirely relieved by federal and state laws. Legislators passed the laws in large part so that fears over privacy loss or criminal prosecution would not keep alcoholics/addicts from seeking treatment. The two governing federal laws are the Comprehensive Alcohol Abuse and Alcoholism Prevention, Treatment, and Rehabilitation Act of 1970 and the Drug Abuse Prevention, Treatment, and Rehabilitation Act of 1972.

Current regulations under these laws essentially require that any communications concerning treatment for alcohol or drug abuse with personnel providing such treatment shall remain strictly confidential. Such confidentiality parallels the confidentiality applying to the privileged communications between doctor and patient, or lawyer and client. Those regulations are in the Code of Federal Regulations.

- ### Types of Treatment Programs

You face what at first seems to be a bewildering variety of treatment programs offered for alcoholics/addicts. Yet it is often persons like you, rather than the alcoholics/addicts themselves, who must make the decisions about which programs to enter.

In many practical situations, the decision about which program to join is made on the basis of a recommendation by the alcoholic's/addict's doctor or spiritual counselor. Or by a relative or friend (perhaps one in AA or Al-Anon). Or by an intervention counselor, if one has been used. Or (especially these days) by the alcoholic's/addict's HMO or other health insurance carrier. The program choice may also be settled in large part simply by location or available money.

If you do have some choices, and in order to understand a choice that's been made, here are the main types of treatment programs provided today.

Inpatient or Outpatient Detox: Most often, detoxification is done in a hospital inpatient facility (or in a hospital-like section of a separate treatment center for alcoholism/addiction). If in a general hospital, detox is often carried out in either the psychiatric section or in a separate detox section. An alcoholic/addict who has serious medical needs besides detoxification may be treated in a hospital's medical or surgical section while also being detoxed. Inpatient detoxification usually runs three to five days if there are no medical complications.

Outpatient detoxification has been used increasingly in recent years (for obvious cost reasons). Outpatient detox is provided through a doctor's office or clinic setting, with the alcoholic/addict making frequent visits to the doctor. Before starting in any outpatient detoxification, an alcoholic/addict should be given a thorough medical screening to guarantee his or her safety. In many cases, outpatient detox will be combined with an intensive outpatient counseling program requiring daily visits for group or individual counseling.

Close medical monitoring is critical with either inpatient or outpatient detoxification. Reactions while withdrawing from heavy alcohol or drug use can sometimes be fatal.

Outpatient or Inpatient Rehab: Two to four weeks or more of professional treatment after detox are often recommended for alcoholism/addiction. Such treatment is commonly called *rehabilitation* treatment, or simply *rehab*. Inpatient rehab treatment lasting at least four weeks became very widely practiced in the 1980s. (In such inpatient treatment, patients, of course, live at the treatment facilities.) Today, the stay is often reduced to perhaps just two weeks. Intensive daily outpatient rehab treatment extending four weeks or usually far longer has become predominant.

Celebrities and the wealthy whom the media trumpet as getting help with an addiction problem most often go for four-week inpatient treatment at a rehab setting that specializes in recovery from addictions. Perhaps the best-known of these is the Betty Ford Center in Rancho Mirage, California. As noted in chapter 1, this is the alcoholism/addiction treatment center founded by the wife of U.S. President Gerald Ford after she recovered from her own alcoholism/addiction.

The Betty Ford Center and other leading alcoholism/addiction treatment centers often have landscaped grounds and handsome buildings. Also widely known are the Hazelden Foundation in Minnesota (and in Florida, Illinois, and New York), Smithers Alcoholism Treatment Center in New York, Edgehill Newport in Rhode Island, Father Martin's Ashley in Maryland, and Brighton Hospital in Michigan. Less widely known but similarly specialized treatment centers (and ones that are, in general, similarly effective) number in the hundreds and are located throughout the United States.

Hospitals with Special Inpatient Rehab Units: Inpatient rehab treatment for alcoholism/addiction running two to four weeks or more is also offered by a number of general and psychiatric hospitals. In either case such inpatient rehab treatment will typically be housed in a special part of the hospital for the rehab program.

One other type of addiction treatment program which houses the addict on the premises of the facility differs from typical inpatient rehab programs, especially in duration. This other type of residential treatment runs six months or more, and it restricts the patient's actions in many ways. It is generally called the "therapeutic community" type of treatment. This treatment tends to be quite special in the kinds of difficult addicts it serves, and in its methods. It is accordingly described separately in this book, in chapter 6.

Diverse Outpatient Rehab Programs: In outpatient rehab trea.
for alcoholism/addiction, patients do not live at the treatment facilities during treatment, but attend only during specified day or
evening hours. Such outpatient rehab treatment is also often offered
by each of the types of places previously described, that is, by

- specialized treatment centers for alcoholism/addiction
- general hospitals
- psychiatric hospitals

In addition, outpatient rehab treatment for alcoholism/addiction
is provided by many more organizations that specialize in such
treatment. These organizations use various descriptions in their
names, among them *center, board, institute, foundation, service* or
services, program, counselors, group, or *council.*

Essentially, these are counseling organizations that specialize in
treating alcoholics/addicts. Their key operating staff members are
counselors certified by the state in treating alcoholism/addiction
(substance abuse or chemical dependence). They also have affiliated
psychiatrists and physicians. They operate in buildings with offices
for individual counseling sessions, and conference rooms for group
presentations and group therapy sessions.

[Finding and Selecting Treatment Programs]

Once you know something about the main types of programs
(which were just described), you'll be in a good position to find and
get in touch with suitable treatment programs for your alcoholic/
addict. You'll also be in a good position to start evaluating any

you by relatives or friends, or by an inter-
HMO.

Own: Here are two quick ways to search out pos-
rehab treatment programs on your own. (You could,
of   se these tactics in addition to the ones noted earlier in
this chap.er.)

Phone the following toll-free number anytime (twenty-four
hours a day, seven days a week), from anywhere in the country: 1-
800-729-6686. This is the number for the Alcohol and Drug Abuse
Hotline operated by a branch of the U.S. Department of Health
and Human Services in Rockville, Maryland. The service representative, to whom you'll be referred when you telephone, will respond
to your call: when you ask about treatment offerings in your locale,
that person will consult a national directory of offerings. With it,
he or she will give you essential information about the alcoholism/
addiction treatment programs available in your area.

The directory includes only programs licensed or otherwise similarly certified by their state governments. Your information would
include phone numbers so that you'll be able to reach any of the
programs directly. You can also obtain much information about
alcoholism/addiction from this hotline.

A privately operated National Drug and Alcohol Referral Hotline also provides treatment program information for all parts of
the United States (and operates twenty-four hours a day, seven days
a week). This is its toll-free number: 1-800-252-6465.

This hotline provides much the same information about local
treatment programs as the federally operated hotline above. It is
furnished as a public service by an alcoholism/addiction treatment
facility in Massachusetts, the Adcare Hospital of Worcester. Other

private treatment centers, such as ones in Illinois and California, help with providing the hotline service.

• Detox/Rehab Treatment Programs on the Internet

Instead of phoning the national hotline (above) to find treatment programs, you can access its entire directory of such programs on the World Wide Web (http://wwwdasis.samhsa.gov/UFDS/welcome.htm).*

This Web site will give you access to the complete and current listings—of some 11,300 treatment facilities throughout the United States and its territories—in a directory that is also published as a book. It is the *National Directory of Drug Abuse and Alcoholism Treatment Programs, 1998* (compiled by the Office of Applied Studies, Substance Abuse and Mental Health Services Administration, U.S. Department of Health and Human Services; Rockville, MD, 1999).

Accessing this Web site brings you to a page headed "Substance Abuse Treatment Facility Locator." That Web page offers three ways to search for alcoholism/addiction treatment programs: Simple Search, Advanced Search, and Browse. The Simple and Advanced Search features give you both a list of treatment programs in the vicinity of a town or city and state (or a U.S. postal ZIP code) you name, and a road map showing you their locations.

Your list of treatment programs would give, not only the program's name, address, and phone number, but a listing of its major features (such as detox and whether it's inpatient or outpatient, types of rehab treatment, whether the program operates in a hos-

---

*There is no period after the *www* in this URL. The lack of a period is *not* a typographical error.

pital or a separate facility, and what types of health insurance are accepted for payment).

The Browse function provides you with a list of all treatment programs in any geographic area or areas you specify. If you wish, it can also give you a selected list of only such treatment programs having particular features you specify.

As an example, accompanying pages present such a listing of all the alcoholism/addiction treatment facilities for San Jose, California, in the heart of Silicon Valley (headed: *"Name"; "Address"; "Phone"; on pages 60–62*). No selection for facilities with particular features was specified for this listing, so it includes all facilities in the directory for San Jose. The page following the facilities listing, headed *"Key,"* identifies the meaning of abbreviations for features given at the end of the listing for each facility.

• What to Ask About a Treatment Program

You will of course want to determine whether a potential treatment program for your alcoholic/addict had the basic characteristics needed in his or her case. For instance, you might want to be sure it had such features as

- a workable location;
- detox treatment for the specific drugs and/or alcohol involved;
- rehab treatment continued directly after detox;
- treatment costs that accommodate your health insurance or financial situation (some treatment centers base charges on ability to pay, or can otherwise have low costs);
- treatment specially designed for adolescents (if needed by your alcoholic/addict); and

• inpatient or outpatient treatment to satisfy recommendations by a doctor or counselor you have consulted.

Other basic program characteristics you might want to ascertain in a treatment program are suggested by the illustrative "KEY" list identified above. You could find out about all the features listed in this KEY when you phoned the U.S.-operated hotline, or searched its online directory on the World Wide Web.

• *Visit the Treatment Programs and Ask Questions*

After you've gotten initial leads on treatment programs that seem right, visit one or more if at all possible. If not, at least get firsthand information by telephone.

Confirm any answers about program features you've already gotten, in case changes may have been made. Ask any questions that come to mind once you're talking directly with people at the program. Look around and see what it's like. Get the feel of the place and of the people there.

Either in person or on the phone, you should ask what licensing and accreditation the treatment agency holds. These assure that it meets at least minimum standards. Make certain the agency is state-licensed, and ask what type of license it has. Licensing is issued by the government branch responsible for the state's work in alcoholism/addiction. In New York, for instance, that branch is the Office of Alcohol and Substance Abuse Services (OASAS).

Accreditation of alcoholism/addiction treatment centers is national, and is made by two organizations. JCAHO accreditation means that the facility is accredited by the Joint Commission on Accreditation of Health Care Organizations. CARF accreditation

Addiction-Free

Name	Address	Phone	Click on *Services* for code definitions
ACT Consulting Services	2901 Moorpark Avenue Suite 294 San Jose, CA 95128-2505	(408) 248-9011	TX/IO/AD DD/SS SG/PI
ARH Recovery Homes Treatment Options	2345 and 2355 Mather Drive San Jose, CA 95116	(408) 926-2666	TX OS/RR/SS TC CJ
ARH Recovery Homes House on the Hill	9505 Malech Road San Jose, CA 95138	(408) 463-0942	TX OS/RR/DD PW/SS TC/PI
ARH Recovery Homes Inc Mariposa Lodge	9500 Malech Road San Jose, CA 95151	(408) 463-0131	TX OS DT/RD RR/DD HV PW/SS
Adult and Child Guidance Center Compadres Program	950 West Julian Street San Jose, CA 95126	(408) 292-9353	TX PV OS/OR/AD HV/SS CM CO
Adult and Child Guidance Center Compadres Program	380 North 1st Street Suite 200 San Jose, CA 95112	(408) 288-6200	TX PV OS/OR/AD HV/SS CM CO/MD
Alert Driving Inc (ADI) Advanced Drug Diversion Institute	3150 Almaden Expressway Suite 145 San Jose, CA 95118	(408) 445-0491	TX PV OS/OR/DD HV/SS
Alexian Associates Family Psychology and Counseling	3110 Provo Court Suite A San Jose, CA 95127-1034	(408) 272-4321	TX PV OS/OR/AD/SG
Asian American Recovery Services	1370 Tully Road Suite 501 and 502 San Jose, CA 95122	(408) 271-3900	TX PV OS/OR IO/AD/SS
Asian Americans for Community Involvement	2400 Moorpark Avenue Suite 300 San Jose, CA 95128-2680	(408) 975-2730	TX PV OS/OR/AD DD/CM SC CJ
Benny McKeown Center	1281 Fleming Avenue San Jose, CA 95127	(408) 259-6565	TX OS/RR/DD HV/SS

The Professional Way

Name	Address	Phone	Click on *Services* for code definitions
Blossoms Perinatal Center Gardner Family	3030 Alum Rock Avenue San Jose, CA 95127	(408) 254-3396	TX PV OS/IO/PW/ SS/FG
Central Treatment and Recovery Center	976 Lenzen Avenue First Floor San Jose, CA 95126	(408) 299-7280	TX OS/OR/DD/SS/ MD
Central Valley Methadone Clinic	2425 Enborg Lane San Jose, CA 95128	(408) 885-5400	TX ML PV OS DT/ OD OR IO/DD HV PW/SS/MD
Charter Behavioral Health System of San Jose	455 Silicon Valley Boulevard San Jose, CA 95138	(408) 224-2020	TX PV OS DT/OR IO ID/AD DD/PH/ MC MD PI
Columbia Good Samaritan Hospital Recovery Center	2425 Samaritan Drive San Jose, CA 95124	(408) 559-2000	TX OS DT/OR IO ID/DD/GH/PI
Combined Addicts and Professionals Services (CAPS) Residential Unit	398 South 12th Street San Jose, CA 95112	(408) 294-5425	TX OS/RR/PW/SS TC
Combined Addicts and Professionals Services (CAPS)/ Outpatient Program	693 South 2nd Street San Jose, CA 95112	(408) 995-3820	TX OS/OR/SS
Drug Abuse Treatment	2220 Moorpark Avenue San Jose, CA 95128	(408) 885-5400	TX ML OS DT/OD OR/PW/SS/MD
East Valley Treatment and Recovery	1675 Burdette Drive Suite B San Jose, CA 95121	(408) 270-2587	TX/OR/DD/SS/MD
Economic and Social Opportunities Inc Rehab Health Services	1445-1447 Oakland Road San Jose, CA 95112	(408) 289-1070	TX PV OS/OR/AD HV/SS
Fortunes Inn ARH Recovery Homes	52 South 12th Street San Jose, CA 95112	(408) 293-6372	TX PV OS/RR/HV/ SS TC HH CJ
Horizon Services Horizon South	650 South Bascom Avenue San Jose, CA 95128	(408) 283-8555	TX OS DT/RD RR/ DD/SS

Name	Address	Phone	Click on *Services* for code definitions
Indian Health Center of Santa Clara Valley Inc	1333 Meridan Avenue San Jose, CA 95125	(408) 445-3400	TX PV OS/OR/AD DD PW/CH
National Traffic Safety Institute	275 North 4th Street 2nd Floor San Jose, CA 95112	(408) 297-7200	TX PV OS/OR/SS
Office of Children Adolescent and Family Services (OCAFS)/Foothill	230 Pala Avenue San Jose, CA 95127	(408) 299-2304	TX PV OS/OR/AD DD/SS SC/MD
Pate House Recovery Home	35 South 12th Street San Jose, CA 95112	(408) 295-4143	TX PV OS/OR IO RR/DD/SS OH TC
Pathway House	102 South 11th Street San Jose, CA 95112	(408) 244-1834	TX OS/RR/SS TC/ FG
Proyecto Primavera Garner Family Care Corporation	614 Tully Road San Jose, CA 95111	(408) 977-1591	TX PV OS/OR/SS CO
Support Systems Homes Inc Support Systems Homes III	1032 Thornton Way San Jose, CA 95128	(408) 370-9688	TX OS/OR IO RR/ SS HH CJ
Willow Home	808 Palm Street San Jose, CA 95110	(408) 294-5072	TX PV OS/IO RR/ DD/SS TC CJ

indicates approval by the Commission on Accreditation of Rehabilitation Facilities. Either or both of these accreditations is often
required for funding of treatment by an HMO.

• *Dual Diagnosis Treatment*

You may need to ask about "dual diagnosis." As many as half of all
Americans afflicted by mental illness also suffer from alcohol-

---

KEY

Facility Function

TX-Substance abuse treatment
ML-Methadone/LAAM
PV-Primary prevention
OS-Other substance abuse services
DT-Detoxification services

Type of Care

OD-Outpatient detoxification
OR-Outpatient rehabilitation
IO-Intensive outpatient rehabilitation
ID-Hospital inpatient detoxification
IR-Hospital inpatient rehabilitation
RD-Residential detoxification
RR-Residential rehabilitation

Facility Setting

SS-Facility that specializes in substance abuse treatment
GH-General hospital
PH-Psychiatric hospital
OH-Other specialized hospital
TC-Therapeutic community
HH-Halfway house
CM-Community Mental Health Center or other mental health facility

CH-Community Health Center, Migrant Health Center, Urban Indian Program, Health Care for the Homeless Center
CO-Community or religious organization/agency
SG-Solo or group practice
SC-School
CJ-Criminal justice or correctional facility

Third Party Payments

MC-Medicare
MD-Medicaid
FG-Federal government (includes VA, CHAMPUS, CHAMPVA)
PI-Private insurance (includes fee-for-service and HMO/PPO/managed care)

Special Programs

AD-Adolescents
DD-Dually diagnosed
HV-Persons with HIV/AIDS
PW-Pregnant and postpartum women

Services offered at the individual facilities may have changed since the information used in this directory was compiled. Please call the provider to verify that the information is current.

---

ism/addiction, studies have found. (Some authorities surmise that alcohol and/or drugs may relieve the symptoms of the person's mental illness, at least at the start.) It may be that the alcoholic/addict you care about also suffers from a mental illness that has been professionally diagnosed, such as bipolar disorder or clinical depression. If so, you would want to make sure that a treatment center for alcoholism/addiction also offers accompanying assessment and treatment for the addict's mental illness. Such patients have a dual diagnosis of both chemical dependence and another mental illness. Any possible treatment programs for your alcoholic/addict should offer specific services for the dually diagnosed.

How to promote recovery from addiction for a dual diagnosis alcoholic/addict is discussed further in the last chapter of this book.

• Answering Their Questions

When visiting or phoning for details, expect to be asked important questions in turn by those at the treatment center. Most vitally, those questions would concern the alcoholic/addict for whom you're seeking treatment. Quite a lot of key details about her or him would bear on what kind and extent of treatment seemed needed. Such details could determine whether that center could serve the particular alcoholic/addict well, what types of treatment might be recommended, or even how effective the treatment would eventually prove.

To apply such details about admitting a potential patient systematically, a treatment center would very likely follow a special set of standards. These are the Patient Placement Criteria issued by the professional society of physicians who specialize in alcoholism/addition, the American Society of Addiction Medicine.

Other questions you'd probably be asked by persons at a prospective treatment center would concern practical matters—tentative starting dates, insurance coverage, payment arrangements, and so forth.

New Professional Ways to Help Start an Alcoholic/Addict on Recovery

Besides the intervention method, several other innovative counseling techniques might help get your alcoholic/addict into recovery. Like the intervention method, these new approaches attempt to help the alcoholic/addict start recovery early, before all the years of agony and loss that might otherwise pass before he or she hits bottom. One of these approaches could appeal to you as simpler or more promising than intervention of the Johnson Institute type.

Two such approaches are outlined here. Either method would be offered in sessions with an individual counselor providing therapy to the alcoholic/addict. The two approaches are

- motivational interviewing; and
- network therapy.

• Motivational Interviewing

Much counseling therapy for alcoholism/addiction in the past sought to confront the client's denial head-on. In this respect, it resembled intervention of the Johnson Institute type, seeking to break through denial much as hitting bottom would, but much sooner. Often, though, the confrontation generated ever stiffer resistance.

By contrast, conflict within the alcoholic/addict rather than from outside is used in motivational interviewing. This method uses special procedures and techniques to work with this inner conflict to help develop the client's own motivation to stop drinking/drugging and begin recovery.

Of course, you'd first need to get your alcoholic/addict to agree to meet with a counselor in order for motivational interviewing to start. Counseling is agreed to in some cases. Alcoholics/addicts nearing their bottoms feel they have many problems, of love life or family or work or money or nameless fears. Possible counseling help with problems like these may at times prove welcome to them. They may even be persuaded to see a counselor to prove they don't have a problem with alcohol or drugs.

Right at the start, a counselor applying the motivational interviewing (MI) method would determine that your alcoholic/addict was in one of three main stages regarding recovery. The stages form a progression, and the aim of MI is to move the alcoholic/addict through each stage, eventually entering recovery:

1. Not ready (to start recovery) ► 2. Unsure ► 3. Ready

How the MI counselor might do this successfully is described by entire books and training programs. Very briefly, though, the counselor respects the client's motivation and thoughts reflecting the client's stage at that time. The counselor always avoids telling the client what to do. Instead, the counselor encourages the client to talk about his or her drinking and/or drugging, and how it may be affecting important aspects of life. Thoughtfully listening represents an important element in MI.

Invariably, an alcoholic/addict will talk of discrepancies between what he or she wants in such areas as health, finances, family life, work, or even physical safety, and what consequences drinking or drugging brings to these areas. Sympathetically but repeatedly reminding the client of those discrepancies is one of the main ways in which the counselor influences change in the client's motivation.

Another technique is to obtain details about the client's drinking or drugging, and to present objective facts about where the client stands in the whole range of danger and damage due to alcoholism/addiction.

Resistance by the client to continued counseling at any point is said to indicate that the counselor has made a mistake. The mistake has been not to stay in the same stage of motivation progression as the client, but instead to have moved ahead into the next. Resistance fades when the counselor moves back to the appropriate stage.

In time, the alcoholic/addict is guided by the counselor to reach her or his own conclusions about the alcoholism/addiction and what to do about it. This moves the client through the stages of "Not Ready" and "Unsure" into "Ready." In the "Ready" stage, the counselor outlines the options for treatment and recovery open to the client, who will reach her or his own decisions about which treatment or program to enter in order to start on recovery.[1]

• Network Therapy

Another new counseling approach that may facilitate getting recovery started is network therapy, also used in sessions with an individual counselor. However, in it, the alcoholic/addict goes to the therapy sessions with someone he or she feels very close to. For some, this may make it easier than going alone. At a number of the sessions, one or two more people close to the alcoholic/addict sit in regularly in support of the treatment and the alcoholic/addict.

You yourself might might well play a prime supporting role in a network-therapy treatment for the alcoholic/addict. Typical members of the network or support team include such persons as a spouse or lover, a brother or sister, a mom or dad, or a very close friend.

An advantage right from the first treatment session can result from the network therapy approach, according to Dr. Marc Galanter of the Division of Alcoholism and Drug Abuse, School of Medicine, New York University.[2] A leading proponent of the method, Dr. Galanter notes that alcoholics/addicts "may deny or rationalize even if they have voluntarily sought help."

A patient is therefore asked to bring a close friend or spouse along beginning with the very first session. Someone close, Dr. Galanter says, "can often cut through the denial in the way that an unfamiliar therapist cannot." Such a person can prove "essential both to history-taking and to implementing a viable treatment plan." Some patients balk at having a "significant other" present at first, he says, but the counselor should require having another attend after one or (at most) two sessions for the sake of building a "therapeutic alliance" to support recovery.

One or two others close to the alcoholic/addict are added shortly after or even at the first session. Time demands on the network members are not large. They usually attend weekly counselor-patient sessions through the first month or so, and then shift to every other week and later to once a month and once every other month.

Network members function as a team to reinforce the patient's abstinence from alcohol or drugs. They do so by being available for the alcoholic/addict to talk to by phone or in person when the alcoholic/addict is feeling discouraged or having urges for alcohol or drugs. They also help by giving encouragement and by taking part in joint social activities with the patient from time to time.

In addition, they monitor the patient's everyday life and report to the counselor any possible problems they may see developing. Any such reports are aired at a session attended by all. Word of any alcohol or drug use by the patient is also shared among all network members, the patient, and the therapist.

Network members are not the recipients of any therapy themselves (as some might be in programs of therapy for family members related to an alcoholic/addict, discussed later in the chapter). As a result, the counselor only advises network members about their support roles, rather than working in any way to help effect changes in them.

Calling Alcoholics Anonymous a form of network therapy, Dr. Galanter says, "Certainly participation in AA is strongly encouraged" for an alcoholic patient in treatment with network therapy. He adds that "groups such as Narcotics Anonymous, Pills Anonymous, and Cocaine Anonymous are modeled after AA and play a similarly useful role for drug abusers."

• Other Therapy Methods

Not only such newer methods as the foregoing but longer-established ones in psychotherapy might influence your alcoholic/addict to begin recovery. Use of these other methods might start by helping your alcoholic/addict look at other related mental or emotional needs.

For example, alcoholism/addiction often inflicts depression. You might therefore be able to persuade your alcoholic/addict to consult a therapist for help with that. A therapist versed in treating alcoholism/addiction could, in time, present your alcoholic/addict with a convincing diagnosis of alcoholism/addiction. One convincing enough, that is, to lead the alcoholic/addict to try recovery. In a number of cases, exactly this has occurred.

As another example, couples therapy involving both you and the alcoholic/addict might be started. Raging alcoholism/addiction certainly does develop sharp tensions between couples. At sober moments your alcoholic/addict might be talked into trying couples therapy to improve things with you (perhaps even to get you to understand him or her). And couples therapy sessions have on occasion led an alcoholic/addict partner to begin recovery.

[Detox Can Be Essential]

For a late-stage alcoholic/addict, withdrawal from alcohol or drugs—that is, going without them—brings on a set of almost unbearable reactions. These physical and emotional reactions keep alcoholics/addicts addicted. In this stage, the body and brain have become so adapted to the intoxicants of choice that they're needed merely to feel halfway normal.

Not drinking or drugging soon results in painful reactions from many body systems. Hands shake, skin sweats, heart pounds, stomach knots, muscles ache, throat tightens, and terrors, rage, despair, and self-hate run wild. Only alcohol or drugs relieve these agonies, the addicts know. They're driven to do absolutely anything that's needed to get relief, no matter who it hurts or what it costs.

There's no getting high anymore at this stage. There's just getting relief for a little while before the withdrawal furies return. Merely the fear of withdrawal can force the alcoholic/addict to keep on drinking or drugging. A state like this goes on for an indefinite time, and then usually leads to the permanent dementia called "wet brain," or a heart attack, or a hemorrhage in the throat, or convulsions, or jail, or a crippling injury in a fall or car crash, or death.

But there's another way out of the tortures and imprisonment of withdrawal. That way is detoxification.

• *When to Detox*

You might at some time find it critically urgent to get the alcoholic/ addict into a detox facility, as outlined early in this chapter. By now the person is so sickened by alcohol or drugs that he or she asks to see a doctor (or at least doesn't resist seeing one).

Detox could prove just as essential without such critical urgency, however. It could be essential whenever there's a threat of withdrawal reactions, especially a threat of severe reactions. And withdrawal reactions can threaten, of course, whenever an alcoholic/ addict either agrees or decides to stop drinking or drugging. If your efforts to have the alcoholic/addict start on recovery succeed, you should be sure to have a doctor determine whether the alcoholic/ addict needs to detox.

Knowing what might happen without a detox may help you convince your alcoholic/addict to see a doctor for a referral. Withdrawal reactions can begin as the effects of the last drink or drug wear off. They can be acute within twenty-four hours, ranging from severe to fatal.

If the alcoholic/addict survives, withdrawal reactions progress unpredictably, and vary with the substances abused. The most intense reactions last some three to five days for an alcoholic, or as long as three weeks for someone addicted to an opiate like heroin.

Detox is medical treatment to counteract withdrawal reactions in this initial acute phase. It is carried out to combat the dangers and to lessen the agonies of acute withdrawal. Of course, it also helps protect the alcoholic/addict from being driven back to using for momentary relief of the withdrawal symptoms.

Alarming Signs of Withdrawal from Alcohol: Withdrawal reactions are especially hazardous in the case of alcohol. If in acute withdrawal from alcohol, alcoholics/addicts could undergo the following reactions:

- Extreme anxiety, irritability, agitation
- Nausea, vomiting, disgust with food
- Hands shaking so badly they can't hold a glass
- Rapid heartbeat, high blood pressure, fever
- Terrifying nightmares, sleeplessness
- Inability to think, recall, or pay attention
- Painful sensitivity to noises or being touched
- Hallucinations—seeing visions, hearing voices, feeling bugs crawling on the skin
- Paranoid delusions of imminent dangers from anywhere and anyone
- Convulsions that can be fatal from choking on the tongue or on own vomit

Alarming Signs of Withdrawal from Narcotics Like Heroin: Should your alcoholic/addict instead be in the acute stage of withdrawing from a narcotic drug like heroin, he or she would at first have these reactions—fast breathing, sweating, runny nose, teary eyes, dilated pupils, goose bumps, fear and agitation, disgust for food.

But when such narcotic withdrawal reactions become advanced, alcoholics/addicts also experience:

- Sleeplessness
- Nausea, vomiting, diarrhea, sharp abdominal cramps
- Muscle spasms, aching muscles and bones, lack of strength
- Rapid heartbeat, high blood pressure

Alarming Signs of Withdrawal from Tranquilizers or Sedative Drugs: If your alcoholic/addict were withdrawing from a tranquilizer like Valium or a sedative like a barbiturate, you'd see reactions like these in the acute stage of withdrawal:

- Uncontrollable trembling of hands, arms, and other parts of the body
- Nausea, vomiting, disgust with food
- Sleeplessness, terrifying nightmares
- Fever
- Low blood pressure, with dizziness or fainting when suddenly standing up
- Convulsions
- Agitation, even delirium
- Psychotic breakdown, if the drugs had suppressed severe panic or paranoid fears

Alarming Signs of Withdrawal from Crack, Cocaine, or "Speed": Withdrawal reactions of your alcoholic/addict from crack cocaine, cocaine, or "speed" (technically, methamphetamine)—which are stimulant drugs—would include the following:

- Almost hallucinatory dreams alternating with sleeplessness
- Utter exhaustion
- Deep depression, complete hopelessness
- Extreme jumpiness and irritability
- Almost irresistible drug cravings

Such withdrawal reactions typically lessen in two to four days, depending on how much, how often, and how long the alcoholic/

addict drugged. These reactions alone usually don't call for physiological treatment, as do withdrawal reactions for some other substances. But the reactions make the person highly vulnerable to using again. Detox hence would include blocking out such relapse possibilities, plus relieving all possible stress and ensuring needed nutrition and rest.

Alarming Signs of Withdrawal from Other Drugs: Still other drugs could be involved in the withdrawal and consequent detox needs of the addict who concerns you. Such withdrawal reactions and detox needs for a variety of other widely used drugs are as follows:

- Marijuana—irritability for a few days, in some cases
- LSD and other hallucinogens like mescaline, PCP (angel dust, phencyclidine), ecstacy (XTC, MDMA)—no apparent need to counteract physical dependence, but severe psychotic aftereffects in some cases may need psychiatric treatment. Chronic PCP use can cause a toxic psychosis taking days or weeks to clear.
- Inhalants (glue, gasoline, paint, aerosol sprays)—withdrawal reactions similar to those for alcohol, and thus needing similar medical treatment

- *Qualities to Seek in a Detox*

Providing effective and safe detox treatment can be very complex. For an alcoholic/addict, detox is also a difficult and uncomfortable experience at best. Probably the two most important qualities to seek in a detox are these: First, medical capabilities to provide all needed health care for this particular alcoholic/addict. Second, a sense of complete safety and strong encouragement for recovery to the alcoholic/addict.

You might also seek a third quality that's highly desirable, if you can manage it. This is a detox treatment that's structured as part of an overall program of detox with rehab immediately following the detox. An alcoholic/addict can be highly vulnerable to relapse right at the time of leaving detox. Going directly into rehab treatment can substantially increase chances of successful recovery.

Make a decision between inpatient and outpatient detox only on the advice and recommendation of a physician. Outpatient or ambulatory detox, of course, costs much less than inpatient. But it is adequate only for alcoholics/addicts who are less heavily addicted and less plagued by medical difficulties than those who need inpatient detox.

• *What Would Detox Be Like?*

Inpatient Detox: As mentioned earlier in the chapter, inpatient detox would be given in either a hospital or in the hospital-like section of a free-standing residential treatment center for alcoholism/addiction. Hospital care may be entirely appropriate, especially if your alcoholic/addict is at a critical point in this chronic and potentially fatal disease. She or he would also be likely to feel sick all over, frightened, worn out, defeated, hopeless. Just being taken care of and being able to rest in bed should feel very welcome. Moreover, hospital confinement would keep her or him away from any alcohol or drugs during detox treatment.

First comes a detailed intake interview. Having you or someone else close to the alcoholic/addict there to help with the interview and patient history might be needed in order to get all the facts. Alcoholics/addicts starting recovery typically have very poor memories. They may not even be aware of much that they've done, or just what drinks and drugs they've been having. Or, if lucid, they may be defensive and guarded in talking truthfully about their drinking or drugging.

Next would come a thorough medical exam, with any necessary tests and labwork. Ongoing bed rest and medical monitoring would begin.

Medications and any treatment appropriate to the patient's needs are provided. In alcohol detoxification, for instance, very heavy dosages of vitamins, especially the B-complex vitamins, are given to correct the huge vitamin deficiencies that alcoholics develop. Anticonvulsion medicines may also be given. Alcohol cravings and anxiety are often countered by having the alcoholics take a tranquilizer, such as Librium. Tranquilizer dosages usually start high but are reduced on successive days (and ended very shortly, to avoid causing another addiction).

Meals and snacks especially planned to meet the nutritional needs of the patient are an important part of the treatment. Alcoholics/addicts eat very badly if at all while drinking and drugging. They thus start into recovery with many severe nutritional deficiencies that require correcting.

Visits by you and one or two others who care about the alcoholic/addict would be helpful if the tone of the visits can be kept encouraging and optimistic. Short visits after the first day or so might be best if they don't interfere with rest and treatment.

Some counseling (to encourage but especially to inform and guide the alcoholic/addict) may be given. A staff doctor or counselor would very probably be able to recommend an outside rehab treatment program for the alcoholic/addict to enter immediately after leaving the detox (that is, if the detox facility doesn't already provide rehab treatment). In some cases, the detox facility might need to get the patient's written permission in order to give a recommendation for rehab treatment after detox.

Most alcoholics/addicts who leave detox and don't go right into rehab treatment (or AA, or both) soon go back to drinking and drugging again.

Outpatient or Ambulatory Detox: Again, only on sound medical advice should the alcoholic/addict enter an outpatient detox. Severe physical problems (and perhaps psychiatric ones also) of an alcoholic/addict in withdrawal may require the degree of monitoring and range of services available only in a hospital setting.

In outpatient detox, the alcoholic/addict is given much the same kinds of examinations, tests, and treatments as with inpatient. For these, he or she would go every day to a facility like a doctor's office or clinic. Detox treatment would typically be carried out over a period of several days to a week or two. Care would be intensive; if any emergency arose when the patient was not making a doctor's office visit, the patient would be able to call for immediate help.

Meals and nutrition would be controlled as carefully as possible. As much rest as possible would be advised (though some individuals go through outpatient detox while continuing to work or carry on homemaker responsibilities).

Counseling and recommendations for subsequent rehab treatment would also be given. (With the patient's written permission, you, too, might be able to obtain these recommendations.) A number of facilities that offer outpatient detox do so as part of comprehensive detox-and-rehab programs. As a result, should you and your alcoholic/addict arrange for outpatient detox at such a facility, he or she would automatically continue right on into rehab treatment.

• What Would Rehab Be Like?

Inpatient Rehab: Inpatient or residential rehab treatment may be said to represent the classic rehab variety. It has set what is by far the predominant content for rehab treatment in the United States. Studies have shown that the other broad type of rehab—outpatient or nonresidential treatment—proves just about as effective for continued abstinence over a large and diverse group of alcoholics. However, inpatient rehab is widely viewed as more appealing to alcoholics/addicts generally, and more likely to result in ongoing recovery for those very severely addicted.

Your alcoholic/addict starting out in an inpatient rehab program might feel like someone arriving at boarding school—a very special boarding school. He or she would, of course, feel very strange and out of place. It won't help that one of the special differences at a rehab is searches of all the luggage and clothing of new arrivals. Any drugs, and any toiletries containing alcohol (like mouthwash or after-shave lotion), would be removed and locked away.

As in a boarding school, the alcoholic/addict has a set schedule every day, a daily array of specified activities with required attendance, dormitory-style rooms with roommates, and dining-hall meals. The program is likely to include restriction to the rehab grounds throughout the stay (and possible off-limits designations for parts of the grounds), no overnight or weekend visits home, and no visitors except as called for in the program.

At first, your alcoholic/addict might react in very guarded and inwardly suspicious ways to all the strangers encountered there. Of course, everyone there would be a stranger. Your alcoholic/addict is likely to regard fellow patients with even more mistrust than he or she feels toward staff members.

Long-Running Withdrawal Reactions Can Add to Rehab Discomfort: Before rehab, in detox, your alcoholic/addict would have gotten through the acute withdrawal reactions. However, he or she could find that still more withdrawal during rehab is making him or her uncomfortable. He or she might be suffering the symptoms of what is called protracted or post-acute withdrawal. These can continue for weeks or months. They can include intense cravings for alcohol or drugs, along with many physical and emotional difficulties. Among those difficulties may be insomnia, headaches, nagging aches and pains anywhere in the body, extreme mood swings, anxiety, nervous tension, depression, restlessness, and boredom.

Your alcoholic/addict would begin on a very full schedule of daily activities right away. There would be a great deal to be accomplished in relatively little time. Inpatient rehab programs paid for by health insurance today usually run for only some two weeks. Some inpatient rehab facilities offer programs running twenty-eight days, which was the predominant program length throughout the country in recent years.

Basic elements of the scheduled rehab activities would be:

- education (most essentially about the disease of alcoholism/ addiction, and its effects);
- therapy (group and individual therapy, aimed at breaking through denial and changing deep-seated attitudes involving alcohol and/or drugs); and

• behavior change (aimed at having the alcoholic/addict start to act in ways that reinforce abstinence, through education and therapy sessions and also sessions of appropriate exercise, a healthy routine of meals and sleep, and in many cases participation in a twelve-step support group's meetings while in rehab).

Interactions with Others May Have Greatest Impact: Your alcoholic/addict is likely to be affected most profoundly by the experiences and actions of the other rehab patients. Seeing what catastrophes and agonies others had gone through while actively addicted—and what astounding defenses their denial had thrown up—can lead your alcoholic/addict to clearly see the parallels in her or his own life.

Being able to identify with the wretched feelings and disasters of another alcoholic/addict represents a highly effective advance toward recovery. Utter honesty is strongly cultivated in rehab. That bedrock honesty of others and constant close association with them would probably influence your alcoholic/addict to identify his or her own apalling addiction experiences with theirs. Similar honesty, a deep sense of camaraderie, and determination to recover could result.

One or more counselors at the rehab could also very deeply affect your alcoholic/addict. Their professional knowledge of the disease, augmented by their experience in treating many different alcoholics/addicts, could make your alcoholic/addict find some of their insights and advice to be amazingly helpful. A number of counselors are also in recovery themselves from alcoholism/addiction. A counselor like this might make an especially powerful impact on your alcoholic/addict.

"Family" Phase of Rehab Could Involve—and Distress—You: You yourself might become involved in the family portion of rehab treatment for your alcoholic/addict, which involves usually parents, brothers, sisters, spouses, lovers or household partners, adult children, or younger children.

Family days usually come toward the end of rehab treatment. By that time, your alcoholic/addict would have progressed far in being able to face and to talk in total honesty about all his or her drinking and drugging.

The family phase of rehab treatment might run as follows: From the start of rehab, your alcoholic/addict would have been meeting in regular group sessions with other patients and a counselor. Family rehab sessions would be held with at least some of the regular group-session members attending. Also, the regular group-session counselor would preside at the family sessions. Attending the family sessions as well would be the visiting family members of all the regular group members. Earlier, the visiting family members would have had individual preparatory meetings with a counselor.

Opening the family session, the counselor would get one family to go first. The counselor would say that each member of that family should speak in turn. Each member should talk directly to (and even look directly at) the patient concerned, and tell in exact detail how the patient's drinking/drugging actions hurt him or her. The counselor tells the patient to just listen without speaking while each member of the family talks.

In some cases, the counselor has learned that the patient's family knew only a little of the full story of the patient's drinking/drugging. In such situations, the counselor may ask the patient to tell the whole story before the family members talk.

After the visiting members of one family have all spoken, the counselor has the patient respond, and has the family talk together. Then the counselor asks the patient and family members to reach conclusions on what they will do after rehab treatment. Those conclusions center on no more drinking or drugging, and family support for continuing recovery.

This all may sound simple in outline. Actually doing it, though, is usually very hard and painful, both for the family members and the patient. But often tempering the pain is forgiveness asked for and granted. There also can be a sense that their addiction nightmares need never happen again.

As you might imagine, the family phase of rehab treatment seeks to dissipate pent-up rage and resentment that could endanger the patient's recovery after rehab. It also seeks to build family support for recovery and to develop sound post-rehab plans.

Another type of professional treatment for substance abuse involving the family might help you a great deal. It is family therapy designed to help the family members themselves recover from the dysfunction caused by the disease of the family's alcoholic/addict. The alcoholic/addict usually does not take part in such family therapy. It is briefly discussed later in the chapter.

Aftercare Set Before Ending Rehab: A vital step to take before your alcoholic/addict leaves rehab is to plan and get his or her agreement for *aftercare*, continuing treatment and actions like joining an AA group right away after rehab. Aftercare could include therapy sessions with a counselor at frequent intervals. An aftercare counselor might be chosen from the rehab program if the patient lives nearby, or it could be a counselor far away with a connection to the rehab for patient referrals.

Aftercare might also include a provision for one or more return sessions at the rehab facility after every four, six, or more months. Membership in AA (or a similar group) in aftercare would continue the addict's exposure to AA meetings (and continue work on AA's twelve steps that would probably have been begun as part of rehab treatment).

Aftercare including residence at a halfway house for newly recovering alcoholics/addicts may be recommended for some patients leaving rehab. A halfway house is a group residence in a house or apartment with a resident manager or counselor in charge.

A halfway house might be arranged for your alcoholic/addict after rehab if his or her home or old neighborhood threatens to sabotage recovery. Or one might be arranged if she or he needs a subsidized and supportive home while establishing regular employment, clean and sober habits, and straight friends in regular daily life.

Outpatient Rehab: If inpatient rehab resembles boarding school or college, outpatient rehab is like being a commuter to college. In outpatient rehab, the alcoholics/addicts live at home and travel to the rehab facility for their rehab sessions.

Outpatient or nonresidential rehab typically includes the same basic elements as the inpatient variety. Among these elements are group therapy, individual therapy, intensive alcoholism/addiction education, work on behavior change, family rehab meetings, introduction to AA (or another twelve-step group), and in some cases continual medical monitoring.

In addition, outpatient rehab treatment would likely include urinalysis drug-screening. This would detect any possible alcohol or drug use that occurred when the addict was away from the program.

However, almost all outpatient rehab programs run longer than inpatient ones. An outpatient rehab program might last eight weeks or run six months or more.

A main reason for the longer length is that outpatient programs are often attended on a part-time basis. Inpatient rehab programs, by contrast, run full-time through the days and may even include evening sessions.

Your alcoholic/addict, for example, might choose an outpatient program with a schedule meeting her or his needs that is also one recommended by a doctor or counselor. An intensive full-time day program running through both mornings and afternoons might be appropriate if your alcoholic/addict is, as some are, "unemployed and unemployable" at the end of his or her drinking and drugging. At the other extreme, a rehab with long evening sessions several nights a week might work best if your alcoholic/addict has a full-time day job or child-raising responsibilities.

A simple fact about starting in recovery is this: **The longer an alcoholic/addict can be kept from drinking or drugging at the outset of treatment, the higher the chances are that he or she will remain abstinent.**

Therefore, one of the main aims of rehab treatment is simply to keep the alcoholic/addict away from alcohol and drugs for as long as possible. Obviously, inpatient rehab programs tend to be better suited to serve this goal than outpatient ones. As an outpatient, your alcoholic/addict would be exposed to all the temptations to drink or drug that have been there all along.

Being in an outpatient rehab program itself would help counteract such temptations. In addition, were your alcoholic/addict found to be especially shaky, one of two special medications might be recommended.

Antabuse (disulfiram), prescribed by physicians, has been widely used with alcoholics for decades. Usually, the alcoholic takes one Antabuse pill a day (usually in the morning, when recovery resolve is high and temptations are few). It normally has no effect at all. However, if the alcoholic drinks even a tiny amount of alcohol, he or she very soon falls violently ill—nauseated and retching, fevered, sweating, shaking, head-aching, heart-pounding. Such an agonizing reaction can strike for as long as three or four days after the last Antabuse dose. The effect is explained to the alcoholic at the outset. The mere prospect of the reaction often wards off the impulse for a drink.

Not only must Antabuse be prescribed by a doctor, but a doctor should also evaluate the physical condition of your alcoholic/addict in the light of the medication's possible risks. Some individuals may have weak hearts or other conditions that would make potential Antabuse reactions hazardous. Also, while some individuals have taken Antabuse for years with no apparent harm, its possibly deleterious long-term effects are still being studied.

Cravings to Drug or Drink Reduced by Naltrexone: Naltrexone is a second medicine that might be suggested to your alcoholic/addict in outpatient rehab to reinforce abstinence. Its use with alcoholics/ addicts dates only from the latter 1990s, and is still somewhat experimental.

Naltrexone has few if any side effects, and is milder in action than Antabuse. Its major action is to keep opiates like heroin from having any euphoric effect on the addict. In other words, should naltrexone-taking addicts then use heroin, they won't feel any effect—they just won't get high so there is no point in taking the drug.

Naltrexone was more recently found to have similar anti-euphoric effects for alcohol intoxication, and to decrease cravings to drink. It has accordingly begun to be used, somewhat experimentally, with alcoholics.

Of course, Antabuse or naltrexone may be recommended and prescribed by a doctor at any point in recovery (and not only during an outpatient rehab program).

Your alcoholic/addict would be guided into an aftercare program following outpatient rehab. With inpatient rehab, aftercare comes as a relatively sharp break. By contrast, outpatient rehab tends to make a gradual transition into aftercare. Your alcoholic/addict would be likely to move into aftercare mainly by just reducing the number and frequency of group and/or individual therapy sessions.

Rehab for Heroin Addiction: Persons severely addicted to heroin often haven't been able to continue in recovery after rehab treatment of the broad type described so far. As a result, if the person you're concerned about is heavily addicted to heroin, there's a different type of program to consider. This is a methadone maintenance program.

Over decades of use, methadone maintenance has proved more effective in improving the lives of severe heroin addicts than any other type of professional treatment. In a very large proportion of cases, it frees the addict from craving heroin. The addict can thus pursue a normal life in all respects—for example, holding a job, helping in the family, obeying the laws, staying healthy and happy.

Only in one respect is his or her life not normal. Anyone recovering from heroin addiction in a methadone maintenance program takes a methadone dose once a day. At present, methadone can be taken legally only at a special facility authorized to dispense it. An addict would need to go to to his or her methadone center daily and take the dose. Counseling therapy sessions might also be held by the center.

One drawback for your addict would be that methadone maintenance needs to go on indefinitely. Fortunately, though, it has neither immediate nor long-term side effects. It does result in possibly dangerous withdrawal reactions if stopped, calling for a medically managed detox. Another drawback is that methadone maintenance programs tend to be available only in the larger metropolitan areas of the United States. (They are subject to political controversy, and can operate only under heavy regulation by the federal and state governments.)

However, for many thousands of addicts, methadone maintenance provides effective treatment when no other approach seems to do so. Medical authorities have given it unqualified approval. (They also define addiction to heroin and other opiates as a medical disorder needing treatment, rather than a responsibly willed activity.)

Research and experimental clinical trials are being carried out with other medicines that appear to work much like methadone. These medicines in essence block the action of heroin and other opium-derived euphorics in the brain, and are called "opiate agonists." One more that you might perhaps hear of is called LAAM (levo-alpha acetylmethadol). Buprenorphine is a type of agonist being investigated in current research as a possible alternative to methadone.

Family Treatment to Help Heal You and Other Close Family Members

If you are a close family member of the problem alcoholic/addict, getting professional treatment provided for yourself and family members could be valuable in several ways. First, it could influence your alcoholic/addict to start recovery if she or he hasn't already (or at least think about starting). Second, if he or she had begun recovery, it could enable you to act in strong support of that recovery.

Most important, such family therapy could help you recover from the ways in which your own personality had been damaged, perhaps deeply, by the other's addiction. Adults and children living with and depending on an alcoholic/addict live in a world of fear, rage, resentments, lies, frustration, inferiority, self-loathing, and hate. These leave deep-seated emotional scars and poisoned emotional dynamics.

Family treatment seeks to bring understanding of how all these negative developments came about and to relieve all those negative and destructive emotional reactions, replacing them with ones that engender personal well-being and growth. Such treatment often includes recommendations to join Al-Anon (or a similar support organization). Al-Anon grew out of AA and adapted AA's twelve steps. Its members are persons whose lives are affected by an alcoholic, especially one in their family. The next chapter reports on Al-Anon and how it might help you.

Family treatment of this kind is often offered at a number of the organizations providing rehab treatment. You could begin such family treatment for yourself (and perhaps also for the children of the alcoholic/addict) either before or after your alcoholic/addict begins recovery. But the sooner you get started, the sooner you'd know the relief of your own recovery.

[A Landmark Study]

Representing a landmark in its field, a recent research project tested a rather popular theory. The theory held that alcoholism treatment would prove most effective if alcoholics were "matched" with types of treatment programs best fitting their characteristics.

What made this "Project MATCH" study extraordinary were mainly its scale and rigor. Its steering committee of principal investigators consisted of twenty-two doctorate-holding research specialists in the field. It studied 1,726 alcoholics in treatment at nine locations over a three-month period and made follow-up analyses of the alcoholics every three months through the fifteenth month (and after thirty-nine months, for alcoholics among them who had been outpatients).

Those 1,726 alcoholics were randomly assigned among three types of treatment programs: "Twelve-Step Facilitation Therapy" (treatment essentially giving patients an intensive introduction to AA), "Motivational Enhancement Therapy," and "Cognitive Behavioral Therapy."

"Twelve-Step Facilitation" Gives Best Results: Findings possibly helpful to you are as follows (among a great many findings of the Project): First, the results of treatment were "excellent in all three treatment groups," according to a Project report. [3] Also, the study

found "relatively few outcome differences among the three treatments." These and other findings indicate that matching may have only minor effects.

However, among the study's outpatients, abstinence from the fourth through the fifteenth follow-up months was achieved by 24 percent of those treated with "Twelve-Step Facilitation Therapy," compared to 14 percent in the "Motivational" and 15 percent in the "Cognitive" program types. Thus, the "Twelve-Step" program type should bring higher chances of achieving abstinence.

Moreover, alcoholics who completed any of the three programs and then went on into AA attendance had higher "positive client outcomes"—that is, higher rates of successful recovery—than did the alcoholics who did not go on into AA after treatment.

[Treatment Costs]

Costs of professional care for the alcoholic/addict worrying you should not for a moment keep you or the alcoholic/addict from getting treatment. For one thing, treatment often is provided without charge to those who have no money to pay for it. (Payment is made through government subsidy or private charity.)

But one fact is much more important, even if only some money is available to pay for treatment: You can be certain the alcoholism/addiction will over time cost far more than any possible treatment unless the alcoholic/addict starts upon and stays in recovery.

Understanding this, you might be interested to know what some of the major types of treatment for your alcoholic/addict might cost. Here are figures currently given for employers by the Substance

Abuse and Mental Health Services Administration of the U.S. Government:[4]

- ### For Inpatient Rehab Treatment
Inpatient rehab treatment at a rehab center or special hospital unit running some twenty-eight days is usually charged in one all-inclusive fee. Such fees usually range from $3,000 to as high as $20,000 or more.

- ### For Outpatient Rehab Treatment
A single, all-inclusive fee is also often the customary charge for intensive outpatient rehab treatment. For such treatment of one to three months, the flat charge can typically run from $2,000 to more than $8,000.

- ### For Group Counseling Treatment
For treatment in group counseling sessions—a less intensive type of treatment than outpatient rehab—charges are often made on a per-session basis. Such group counseling can frequently be the form of treatment used for aftercare following rehab. Per-session charges customarily range from $25 to $60 or more per session per group member.

- ### For Individual Counseling Treatment
Individual counseling may be used to help motivate the alcoholic/addict to begin recovery, or in aftercare, or in family therapy for someone like yourself. Such counseling is typically charged on a per-session basis, with a session running approximately one hour. Charges per session are usually from $50 to $100 or more.

[*Three*]

The Al-Anon Way: To Stop Enabling;
To Detach with Love

Very special importance may attach to one further major avenue for trying to help the alcoholic/addict who concerns you. A parallel organization to AA, this avenue is officially called Al-Anon Family Groups. Usually, people just say Al-Anon.

You'll probably be shocked and understandably angry to be told that you yourself may be one of the main influences reinforcing the addiction of your alcoholic/addict. However, one of Al-Anon's prime discoveries was this: **Alcoholism almost always forces those closest to the alcoholic to act unknowingly in ways that strengthen the grip of his or her addiction.**

Why? Essentially, because immediate family members and best friends don't realize that the person they care about has developed a disease. And they don't see how the other's addiction has affected the whole way that they themselves feel and react—perhaps very deeply.

In their ignorance, these lovers, spouses, parents, children, or friends help the alcoholic/addict deny or escape the crises caused by the addiction. They tell lies about sickness as the reason for missed days at work. They repeat or even make up excuses about car accidents or injuries or fistfights or arrests. They forgive the alcoholic/addict for not showing up at birthdays or graduations or funerals—or showing up intoxicated. They believe the sincere pledge of the alcoholic/addict that "it won't ever happen again." They pay bills, make loans, and post bail with money they themselves might need badly because the plight of the alcoholic/addict seems so desperate. Of course they're sure that the drinking or drugging will stop.

Sadly, they do all this with the best of intentions, and the most understandable intentions. They hope their caring will make things better. Also, they fear embarrassment with friends and even possible loss of a job by the alcoholic/addict—and consequently a loss of financial support. They may also gloss over crises to protect the children.

In time, they find that excessive drinking or drugging not only continues—it gets worse. They grow angry, bitter, resentful, and constantly fearful about what disappointment or disaster will happen next. They stop having friends visit their home out of shame and embarrassment. They dread the thought of when the alcoholic/addict will come home—and when she or he doesn't come home at all. At times they shout in fury at the alcoholic/addict. He or she shouts back that all this nagging and blaming actually causes the drinking or drugging.

What has happened, on the one hand, is that the addiction has led those around the alcoholic/addict to shield her or him from the consequences of the addiction. But those consequences are what might, quite powerfully, open the way to recovery.

On the other hand, the addiction has made those around the alcoholic/addict so hostile and enraged that the alcoholic /addict feels ever more guilt-ridden, and hence feels ever greater needs for intoxicated relief.

Al-Anon Can Help You Be Part of the Solution

Al-Anon provides a means to break this hideously descending spiral that traps the alcoholic/addict and those who care about him or her. Through it, you can introduce the possibility of recovery for the alcoholic/addict into the hopeless situation in three major ways:

1. By changing your reactions from ones that reinforce addiction to reactions that combat addiction. In Al-Anon, a frequent term for reactions that reinforce addiction is *enabling*. Any reaction of yours that shields the alcoholic/addict from the consequences of the addiction enables him or her to continue in the addiction. Al-Anon can help you see ways in which you enable and can give you many examples of how to stop enabling.

2. By introducing knowledge of alcoholism/addiction and how to recover from it into your life and that of the alcoholic/addict. Without Al-Anon, you would probably stumble on blindly, falling into the fiendish traps that addiction sets for the addict and those close to her or him. But in Al-Anon you could learn the truth about alcoholism/addiction as a disease, how to recognize it, how to deal with it effectively and, most important, with true compassion.

3. Most important in the general view of Al-Anon, you yourself could find a way to recover from the great many ways in which *your* life has been made miserable by your part in alcoholism/addiction. You could learn ways to become free of the fears, the rage, the shame, the embarrassment, and

the resentments suffered by those involved with an alcoholic/addict. And you could learn how to gain such relief and peace of mind whether or not the alcoholic/addict entered recovery.

In Al-Anon you will find you are no longer alone by meeting women and men who face the same trials and terrors as you, and who have learned how to cope with them. These women and men can understand how you feel because they've felt the same way themselves. They would help you change from being part of the problem to being part of the solution, and some would very probably become your close and completely understanding friends.

Find Al-Anon Even If You Merely Suspect Alcoholism/Addiction

Al-Anon should be especially helpful to you even if you're not sure that this person in your life may be addicted to alcohol or drugs. "If you are concerned with someone else's drinking, the Al-Anon program can help you," states an introductory pamphlet, *This Is Al-Anon.*[1]

It might be most helpful to hear what others in situations like yours tell about their experience. Their stories would describe how they came to find out that they faced actual alcoholism/addiction. From this, you could see if experiences of yours that worry you compare with those they've had.

You could also talk about your disturbing experiences due to another's drinking or drugging in Al-Anon meetings. You'd very likely find it a relief just to be able to talk about it with people who can really understand. And you could start to learn how to deal with such difficulties from what the others tell of their own experience, and in talking informally with them before and after meetings.

Al-Anon pamphlets and books that would be offered you at meetings could also shed light on whether there's a serious problem with liquor and drugs. You might conclude that there isn't, after learning all you can with an open mind and going regularly to meetings for perhaps eight or ten weeks. However, in view of the power of denial in those involved with alcoholics/addicts, it's far more likely that you'd conclude the problem to be worse than you'd thought.

• *You Can Probably Find Al-Anon Close to Home*

Al-Anon groups should be functioning right in your own community or neighborhood, or nearby. The most certain way to discover groups in your locale is by contacting Al-Anon's World Service Office. (It's also called Al-Anon Family Group Headquarters.)

To Contact Al-Anon
In the United States: 1-888-425-2666 (1-888-4AL-ANON)
Spanish: 1-800-939-2770
Canada: 1-800-443-4525

A live person will give you meeting information at these toll-free numbers on Monday through Friday every week between the hours of 8:00 A.M. and 6:00 P.M. Eastern Time (Standard or Daylight Time) in North America. A recorded message is given at other hours.

Al-Anon Family Group Headquarters, Inc.
1600 Corporate Landing Parkway
Virginia Beach, VA 23454-5617
U.S.A.
Phone: 757-563-1600
Fax: 757-563-1655
Web site: http://www.al-anon.alateen.org
E-mail: wso@al-anon.org

You might also find Al-Anon groups listed in your local phone directory. A local phone directory listing for Alcoholics Anonymous may also put you in contact with someone knowledgeable about local Al-Anon groups. (Al-Anon meetings are sometimes held at the same locations as AA meetings, though completely separate from the AA meetings.)

• *Your First Meeting*
Once you've gotten a local phone number for Al-Anon, you may feel odd or self-conscious about just showing up by yourself shortly before a meeting starts. If so, you might ask when you phone if a member might take you to your first meeting, or instead at least be asked to greet you there. Members gladly volunteer to do this for newcomers.

Of course, if you've been going to Open Meetings of AA as suggested in chapter 1, you might ask others at those meetings about an Al-Anon meeting in the area. Persons who may have mentioned relatives attending Al-Anon in telling their stories should be able to help you. Those with the longest years sober in AA might also know of Al-Anon meetings nearby.

At an Al-Anon meeting, you're likely to be able to learn of Al-

Anon meetings at other times and locations in your vicinity. Many Al-Anon groups have lists of such other meetings on hand. If a group you try does have such a list, the members there could tell you about other meetings.

Knowing of other meetings would make it possible for you to try several and settle on the one most comfortable for you in people, time, and location. It would also provide you with available meetings in addition to those of your favorite group in case those extra meetings could help you.

Meetings are usually identified, incidentally, by their locations, the days of the week they are held, and their starting times. Meetings last for one hour, in many cases. Generally, an Al-Anon group consists of those individuals who meet regularly at the same location (or set of locations) each week. Some 28,000 Al-Anon and Alateen groups operate in more than 112 countries, according to Al-Anon's World Service Office.

[What You'd Find at Al-Anon]

You can relax any apprehensions you may have about attending your first Al-Anon meetings. You will find the people there welcoming and sympathetic; they clearly recall how uncertain and anxious they felt at their own early meetings. They would also recall how comforted they were by the understanding they had soon found.

You would typically see more women than men at an Al-Anon meeting. However, you might be surprised by the variety of ages and apparent backgrounds of those at a meeting. Diverse individuals often join in an Al-Anon group, but the members develop a very close bond through their common experience of having had their lives deeply affected by an alcoholic/addict.

• *Confidentiality*

By principle and custom, Al-Anon members keep confidential the identities of each person who attends meetings and anything that's said at them. They do so out of mutual respect and trust. They also do so in order to be able to talk with complete honesty at meetings, which aids their recovery in many ways. Like AA, Al-Anon takes anonymity as "the spiritual foundation" of its program. Anonymity is further guarded by the use of only the first name or nickname and the initial of the last name to identify members.

• *Cost-Free*

There are no charges whatever. Group costs are defrayed by voluntary contributions, often collected at meetings by the passing of a basket. One dollar is the widely prevalent individual donation at a meeting. However, it is perfectly acceptable to give nothing. Al-Anon is a nonprofit organization. Official Al-Anon books are priced essentially at cost; official pamphlets are free.

• *Informal and Flexible*

You would not be required or even expected to take any particular action in Al-Anon, except as you wished. You could say nothing at first, except perhaps to introduce yourself by giving your first name.

You'd likely find it natural at some point early on to say a little about how your life is or was affected by an alcoholic. And in time, it's almost certain that you'd talk openly and fervently about your difficulties with the alcoholic, and find this very helpful. Virtually everyone does. In more time, you'd probably talk about how you've begun using the better ways to deal with those difficulties, techniques you've begun learning in Al-Anon.

An Al-Anon meeting is typically led by a volunteer experienced member for a specified number of months set by the group. Often, the meeting leader speaks for a short time at the start, and then the members who wish talk briefly in turn. What they say often illustrates how they've used some element of the Al-Anon program to solve problems in their own experience, or tells about some especially painful current trouble with which they need help. The style is informal and flexible. Talk of sympathy and solutions between individuals goes on before and after meetings.

• For Individuals Involved with Drug Addicts

You should feel free to join Al-Anon even though the person worrying you is primarily (or even exclusively) addicted to drugs rather than alcohol. Other members talk in Al-Anon meetings about their experience with the drug addict in their lives.

By principle, Al-Anon states (in its Tradition 3) that: "The only requirement for membership is that there be a problem of alcoholism in a relative or friend."[2] You can therefore be a member if you say that your relative or friend has an alcoholism problem. This is quite true for the vast majority of drug addicts, who also regularly or occasionally use alcohol addictively. It is also quite true if you understand that alcoholism is essentially addiction whether it be to alcohol or drugs. Such an understanding reflects the view increasingly held in medical circles today. Moreover, an understanding like this is increasingly reflected in the membership of AA itself today, as related earlier.

Al-Anon literature continues to mention only alcohol or alcoholism. Doing so reflects loyalty to the organization's time-tested traditions, and a conservative modesty about its effectiveness. But Al-Anon's present membership reflects persons whose lives are deeply affected by drug addiction as well. In many Al-Anon groups, you would find kindred souls if the person troubling you is addicted to drugs. Members of some Al-Anon groups, though, may occasionally react coolly to talk about problems due to drugs rather than alcohol. If so, seek out another, more congenial group.

Recent years saw the formation of an organization for persons with relatives or friends who are drug addicts. It is named Nar-Anon, and is related to Narcotics Anonymous. Nar-Anon groups are far fewer than Al-Anon groups. Information on how you may locate them is given in the final section of this book, in case you might want to consider going to Nar-Anon rather than Al-Anon meetings. Nar-Anon has no connection with Al-Anon; however, its approach is much the same as that of Al-Anon.

• *Specialized Al-Anon Groups—Alateen; Al-Anon's Adult Children*

To serve the needs of certain kinds of persons affected by another's alcoholism, the Al-Anon Family Groups organization includes two types of special groups. They are Alateen, for teenagers, and Al-Anon's Adult Children (AAC), for adult children of alcoholics. Both types of groups practice essentially the same program as followed by the Al-Anon groups. However, each forms its own groups and holds its own meetings in order to concentrate on the particular kinds of experience and difficulties of its members. Listings of Al-Anon meetings usually include listings of Alateen and AAC meetings.

Brace Yourself for Another's Anger When You Join Al-Anon

One of the many tragic facts about alcoholism/addiction is that this disease almost always forces the poor souls it afflicts to fight off any move that might threaten its grip. As a result, the alcoholic/addict in your life may get furious with you as soon as she or he learns you've joined Al-Anon and gets even the least glimmer of Al-Anon's purpose.

* *Whatever It Takes, Keep Going*

For your own sake, do your absolute best not to let anything your alcoholic/addict does or says keep you from going to Al-Anon. You may get repeated outbursts of rage. You may get pleading. You may get actual periods of no drinking or drugging to "prove" that there's no problem. Your Al-Anon friends will tell you how these and more dodges than you can imagine were tried with them.

Your best defenses, your friends may also suggest, should run something like this: Tell your alcoholic/addict that you're going for yourself, that the fact that you go simply doesn't concern him or her, and that you're just not going to talk about it anymore. Al-Anon friends would likely also suggest that you keep on going with determination, and continue saying nothing about it. In time, after you followed such a course, your alcoholic/addict should be too absorbed in her or his own addiction to do anything more than grumble over Al-Anon now and then.

How deeply an active alcoholic/addict resents a close family member going to Al-Anon was once well expressed in a talk given by a typically eloquent speaker at an Open AA Meeting. In describing his ever-darkening drinking days, he told how his wife started attending Al-Anon meetings. In his and many other parts of the country, Al-Anon meetings, and AA meetings, are held in the parish halls of churches ("church basements," in common parlance). "So that was when my wife, Ruth, started going to Al-Anon meetings," said the speaker grimly, "at the Church of Our Lady of Perpetual Revenge."

As this reflects, the addiction disease of your active alcoholic/addict makes him or her unable to see Al-Anon as anything other than condemning, hostile, and threatening. So above all, don't even think of trying to explain Al-Anon as a program to make your life far better, and possibly to help her or him as well. Let time and events make that clear.

[How to Benefit the Most from Al-Anon]

• *Get a Regular Al-Anon Group*
Most important of all for realizing your potential benefits in Al-Anon is to consistently go to meetings of what you choose as your regular Al-Anon group for at least three to six months. This would probably mean making at least one meeting a week, since an Al-Anon group typically meets at the same time and place once a week. (You could, of course, benefit more from going to other meetings besides those of your regular group.)

Having such a regular or "home" group is thought especially worthwhile. Doing so tends to make it easier for you to feel comfortable in the program, and for you and your fellow members to get to know and care about one another.

• *Get an Al-Anon Sponsor Soon*

You will probably hear members mention their Al-Anon sponsors once you start going to meetings. Almost every member has a sponsor, following a custom of long standing, and good sponsors are widely found to be very helpful. It's customarily recommended for a sponsor to be someone with substantial experience in the Al-Anon program, usually at least a year, and with a grasp of the program that the new member admires.

Fundamentally, a sponsor serves as your guide in the Al-Anon program. It is someone who has had painful experiences and current difficulties much like yours, and who has learned ways of using all elements of Al-Anon to surmount them and have a satisfying life. By custom, sponsors don't give advice. They share their experience and let you draw your own conclusions. Sponsors and others in Al-Anon also ideally refrain from giving any type of professional advice—medical, financial, marital, therapeutic. They instead talk of their own and others' experience in being aided by professionals.

One function served by a sponsor is to be the most important Al-Anon person to phone or see at times of crisis or extreme difficulty. Having someone serve this function for you can be especially vital at the start. You'll also be given the phone numbers of other members of your Al-Anon group so that you may reach any of them when you're troubled. Al-Anon members make such offers of help quite willingly. They believe that by helping others, they help themselves. Also, they pass along the kind of help that they themselves got, and still get, from others.

• *You Might Try a Temporary Sponsor*

Once the people in your regular Al-Anon group begin to seem familiar, you might start thinking of whom you want to ask to be your sponsor. Get a sponsor soon, without undue delay. Someone may offer to be your sponsor, or you may have to ask yourself. If you feel unsure of a choice but want to try someone, you could ask her or him to be your temporary sponsor, and see how things work out.

This agreement can be dissolved by either you or the sponsor at any time if either of you feels that the relationship isn't working out well, for whatever reason. Perhaps the most frequent reason for dissolving is that the sponsor cannot be available as promptly or as much as he or she is needed. On the other hand, some members continue to have the same sponsor for many years, and the relationship grows into a rich and very special friendship. Al-Anon sponsorship is similar to sponsorship in AA.

[Vital Al-Anon Skills]

• To Recover Yourself

Once you've started feeling connected in Al-Anon with a regular group and a sponsor, you'll start developing new skills and capabilities. Keeping an open mind would probably be the most important way you can foster your development. Modest efforts to go to meetings and talk to members and try new ways of thinking would also be important. But much of your new development would probably come about just from being with new people and looking at life in a new way. Especially life with an alcoholic/addict.

One of the first new skills you will probably learn is how to see yourself and your situation in true perspectives. You'll come to understand that the alcoholic/addict close to you is a sick person, totally powerless and blind with respect to his or her addiction. You'll recognize how living with the addiction has changed you into being fearful, angry, hopeless, tense, hate-filled, or obssessed with the addict.

• *Take Back Your Life*

Putting the focus on yourself, and no longer on the alcoholic/addict, becomes increasingly vital to you as you hear others tell how they came into Al-Anon with the very same painful feelings as yours. Their examples can show you varieties of concrete ways in which you can take back ownership of your own life, and thus end many painful feelings.

These developments will start you on the recovery from the damage done to your emotional life and your character by the addiction. And Al-Anon makes it possible for you to go on getting better, whether or not the alcoholic/addict enters recovery.

• *Al-Anon Slogans*

Certain sayings set forth in Al-Anon literature and widely used by members might be the first tools of the program to begin bringing you relief. Try not to dismiss the slogans as simple-minded. They work as quick memory-tags for very effective and quite complex ways of coping.

First Things First: Feeling overwhelmed by all the things you need to do commonly troubles newcomers to Al-Anon. When such a sense strikes you, members might suggest that you don't panic. Instead, remember "First Things First" and decide what's the single most important thing to do right now. Then, forget all the others. Do number one. Next, repeat—set number one, and do it. In this way, you need only concern yourself over one thing, not everything. You also get the most important things done.

An overriding application, members might also suggest, is to keep in mind that your supreme First Thing is your recovery. Maintaining your own recovery comes before anything else because without recovery, your misery will worsen. Accordingly, when feeling really overstressed, your very first thing might be to get to an Al-Anon meeting or visit a supportive friend.

Easy Does It: Feeling desperate and driven is also common for Al-Anon newcomers. Beware of letting stress build up. When you're feeling pressured, try to take a deep breath and relax a bit. Tell yourself that "Easy Does It," and go at the situation with a more composed, confident, and effective stance.

"Easy Does It" also applies to flashes of anger: anger at your alcoholic/addict, at yourself, at anyone who is annoying, at infuriating situations. When you begin to feel that rage surging up, pause. Keep your mouth shut. Silently count to five. Silently say, "Easy does it." Take a really deep breath. Then respond in a calm, reasonable way, if at all. The situation may not even be worth bothering about.

Live and Let Live: On the one hand, this slogan urges tolerance. Al-Anon newcomers are often advised especially to give up complaints and tirades aimed at reforming your alcoholic/addict. Tolerate that person's condition as the disease which addiction is. Stop hostile and condemning efforts that can't possibly do anything but intensify the disease. Also, be careful to avoid inflicting your intolerant impulses toward the alcoholic/addict on such innocent bystanders as your children or friends.

On the other hand, the slogan urges good sense. Most people can't help being who they are. By being critical of them and irritated with them, you aren't going to change them at all. That kind of attitude is only going to leave *you* stewing in your own resentments of them.

Let Go and Let God: Soon after starting Al-Anon you'll hear that its program is a "spiritual" one, in important respects. Keep an open mind on this. How you conceive of spiritual values in Al-Anon is left entirely to you. Al-Anon members of no religious faith, as well as of almost every religious faith, find it very helpful to act on spiritual principles as suggested in the Al-Anon program.

Your best way of understanding spiritual principles in Al-Anon is to learn at meetings and in conversations how members use them, and then trying to use them yourself. Reading Al-Anon books and pamphlets would also help. This book can give only a hint of how you might find these spiritual principles useful.

Many actions can be taken to try to get an alcoholic/addict into recovery, as explained in this book, and in a great many cases, these do succeed. But as yet, no doctor or scientist or any authority whatever can predict in any *individual* case when any one alcoholic/addict will start recovery, or even whether he or she ever will. Tragic cases of individuals who never recover despite what anyone does to help can still occur, as illustrated by the case of Senator George McGovern's daughter, Terry, in chapter 1.

Other diseases like Alzheimer's or varieties of cancer also result in unpredictably tragic cases. However, the disease of alcoholism/addiction seems almost uniquely fiendish. It often appears to be no disease at all, but unbelievable and deliberate perversity in the person who has it. On many occasions it seems defeated, only to return worse than ever. It whipsaws its victims with hope and despair again and again, eventually leaving anyone involved with an active case of the disease deeply terrorized.

Using spiritual power to cope with such appalling difficulties represented early discoveries of AA and Al-Anon. These were practical discoveries, not theoretical or scientific ones. Their justification today remains practical. "Try them," newcomers are urged. "They work for us. See if they'll work for you."

"Let Go and Let God," another Al-Anon slogan, can serve as a memory-tag for applications of Al-Anon spiritual principles. One important way for you to apply it is to the alcoholic/addict in your life. "Let go," would be the suggestion. Accept the fact that you're powerless over the alcoholic/addict and the addiction. Let some supreme and benign spiritual power of whatever form you envision ("God as we understood him," in the AA and Al-Anon phrase) take charge of the fate of the alcoholic/addict.

For extreme skeptics, the form of that power may be only their Al-Anon group and the Al-Anon program. This works for them. For others, the forms range from ones in mysticism or science or nature or art to the divinity of their traditional religion.

Apply the concept to any other troubled area in your life where you don't have the power to control the outcome. To draw on the idea of "Let Go and Let God" could help you stop worrying or being critical of yourself concerning this area. Such worry and self-denunciation have often become chronic in Al-Anon newcomers.

• *Your Further Recovery*

After joining Al-Anon, you'll also soon start hearing members talk about the program's twelve steps. It would be worthwhile for you to approach these, too, with an open mind. Over time, you will hear members tell how they developed understanding of each step, and how they use the steps to further their recovery and thereby help their lives get better.

Your sponsor would probably also share with you her or his experience with the steps. It is customary as well for a sponsor to guide a newcomer through understanding and use of the steps. And you could find out more about the steps by reading Al-Anon's explanations of them in its books and pamphlets.

As with the Al-Anon slogans, its twelve steps are based on practical experience rather than theory and experiments in medicine or science. They were adapted by AA's founders and early members from techniques and practices they found effective for promoting recovery from alcoholism. The measures they adapted had arisen in medical experience on the one hand and, on the other, in a Christian evangelical movement of the 1930s called the Oxford Group. Those measures were codified in the first edition of *Alcoholics Anonymous*, published in 1939, and were introduced there with the phrase: "Here are the steps we took, which are suggested as a program of recovery. . . ." That codification continues unchanged today.[3]

On the basis of experience by its founders and early members, Al-Anon similarly adopted the twelve steps as a recovery program for relatives and friends of alcoholics. Al-Anon's steps differ appropriately by only one word in step 12 from AA's program. Successful recovery by at least several million alcoholics/addicts through AA, and many hundreds of thousands of relatives and friends through Al-Anon, testifies abundantly to the effectiveness of these twelve steps. Here are the twelve steps of Al-Anon, followed by an explanation of a few of the ways in which you might find them helpful.

• *How You Might Use Al-Anon's Twelve Steps in Your Own Recovery*
You could best learn about using Al-Anon's twelve steps to improve your life from meetings, your sponsor, other members, and Al-

The Twelve Steps of Al-Anon[4]

1. We admitted we were powerless over alcohol, and that our lives had become unmanageable.
2. Came to believe that a Power greater than ourselves could restore us to sanity.
3. Made a decision to turn our will and our lives over to the care of God *as we understood Him.*
4. Made a searching and fearless moral inventory of ourselves.
5. Admitted to God, to ourselves, and to one other human being the exact nature of our wrongs.
6. Were entirely ready to have God remove all these defects of character.
7. Humbly asked Him to remove our shortcomings.
8. Made a list of all persons we had harmed, and became willing to make amends to them all.
9. Made direct amends to such people wherever possible, except when to do so would injure them or others.
10. Continued to take personal inventory, and when we were wrong promptly admitted it.
11. Sought through prayer and meditation to improve our conscious contact with God *as we understood Him,* praying only for knowledge of His will for us and the power to carry that out.
12. Having had a spiritual awakening as the result of these Steps, we tried to carry this message to others, and to practice these principles in all our affairs.

(continues)

(*Notes:* The phrase in italics in steps 3 and 11 is italicized in the original text. The one word differing from AA's twelve steps appears in Al-Anon's step 12, where *others* replaces *alcoholics.*)

Anon's very extensive reading materials. However, here's a slight idea of how the steps help you in major ways.

First Step—At Last Seeing Your True Situation: Al-Anon's first step could lead you to recognize the true situation you face, in two vital respects: with your alcoholic/addict, and with yourself.

Admitting, as did other Al-Anon members, that "we were powerless over alcohol" (that first milestone of step 1) means that you give up any idea of having any effect on the disease of the alcoholic/addict with any direct actions of yours. You're as powerless over the disease as he or she is.

Accepting this should give you great relief. Most Al-Anon newcomers have been feeling that something they could do would solve all the problems, and that they fail time after time when nothing they try works. They also often feel—and in many cases have been told—that the disastrous drinking/drugging is their fault. But in the first step, when they at last see that there's no direct action of theirs that can work, they see, too, that the disease is not their fault.

Then, admitting with others that "our lives had become unmanageable" (step 1's second part) can put the spotlight on the misery inflicted on your life by the other's disease, and on getting freed from that misery. Both parts open the way to your recovery. Lives and emotions of those closely involved with someone severely addicted are thrown into chaos and confusion. That's unmanageable. Or, as some prefer to put it, unbearable. And it no longer has to be that way.

If You're Powerless, What Power Can Help? You might draw hope from seeing how the second step has worked in the lives of other Al-Anon members, who "came to believe that a Power greater than ourselves could restore us to sanity." They handle their difficulties with an alcoholic/addict in ways that are calm and reasonable, and find many things that are good in their lives. Surely, they have found a power that enables them to be this way.

That greater power for some members is simply the Al-Anon program and Al-Anon members they trust. This works for their recovery. For others, it is also divine power conceived in any way preferred by the individual. You might best develop a sense of such power, and of how to draw on it, through extended experience in Al-Anon and your life.

Once you "came to believe" in your own personal version of this power, you should be able to reap one of the major benefits of step 3, "made a decision to turn our lives and our will over to the care of" that power. Involvement with an alcoholic/addict typically brings enormous amounts of self-pity and obssession with all the losses and harm to oneself wrought by the other's addiction.

Trying to put your life and intentions into the care of your greater or higher power can relieve such obssession with the self, and such sickening self-pity. It can also put into trusted hands the great many other troubles and problems over which you have no power. It can bring you welcome relief, as you "let go and let God" (God, that is, *as we understood Him*"). When it does, your own recovery has well begun.

[To Stop Enabling]

Developing a fair mastery of subsequent Al-Anon steps can not only further your own recovery, it can also tend to promote the possibility of recovery for the alcoholic/addict in your life.

To an alcoholic/addict you're close to, you have certain natural responses. These lead you to help with difficulties caused by liquor and/or drugs. In ignorance of the disease and the fact that your alcoholic/addict has it, you expect each protective action to be your last. Yet you do more and more.

Your lies become more flagrant and frequent in his or her behalf. The money you sacrifice grows ever larger. As the let-downs and embarrassments increase, and the fears and disasters multiply, you agree that it's not all that bad. You accept promises that it won't happen again. You go along wholeheartedly with the addict's desperate assertions that there really isn't any problem. Doing all this, you see yourself as really helping the alcoholic/addict.

• *Protecting the Alcoholic/Addict Doesn't Help*
In Al-Anon, after listening to other members and reading its literature, you'll learn that actions of yours to protect the alcoholic/addict from the results of her or his addiction do not help. Neither does hiding the truth of the addiction, from yourself especially. Your denials of the addiction and your actions to protect the alcoholic/addict from its consequences make it possible, at least in part, for the alcoholic/addict to continue in the addiction and become more and more ravaged by it. Obviously, "enabling" does not help. The more effective your efforts for the addict, the more harm they do. Addiction commonly kills completely ena-

bled addicts. One prime example is the fabled rock music pioneer, Elvis Presley.

• *How Al-Anon's Steps Help You Stop Enabling*

Al-Anon's next steps, from 4 through 7, might help you especially to cease enabling, but that's only a small facet of your potential benefits. The steps and the whole Al-Anon program are for *your* own recovery. Still, an Al-Anon member's practice of the steps undeniably affects the alcoholic/addict in the member's life.

You might be relieved of resentments and anger and guilt in steps 4 and 5. A byproduct of such relief could be less enabling on your part. Step 4 would ask you to make "a searching and fearless moral inventory." The closely related step 5 calls for members to admit "to God, to ourselves, and to another human being the exact nature of our wrongs." That moral inventory is generally expected to lay out all your shameful or regrettable personality traits, and all your admirable or good traits, as honestly as possible. In step 5, members usually meet with their sponsor for a heart-to-heart discussion of the inventory. (Or they may meet with another trusted Al-Anon friend, or an understanding professional like a therapist or clergyperson.)

• *Freedom from Negative Emotions*

This process could bring out into the open many of the negative emotions causing you pain, such as resentments, rage, hate, fear, shame, self-loathing, envy, and disappointment. It could also uncover, on the other hand, such things as your bravery, persistence, loyalty, and ambition. After working through these steps with their sponsors, members often feel relieved of much guilt on their conscience caused by past negative emotions. Further progress can be made by members in the sixth and seventh steps. These aim at removing "defects of character" that give rise to negative emotions.

Habitual ways of reacting can change slowly if you keep up your efforts with these steps. Changing the way you react to the alcoholic/addict in your life could bring you far more confidence and self-respect, less anxiety, more trust, more tolerance, and a much greater understanding of yourself and the alcoholic/addict. As a result, you might no longer lie, sacrifice money, burst out in anger, and clean up after or in any other way protect the alcoholic/addict from experiencing the direct brunt of misfortunes due to his or her addiction. That is, you might stop enabling.

Detach with Love

Further steps would involve you in what might be called advanced Al-Anon. They could help you reach a new plateau in your approach to yourself and to your life—and, of course, your approach to your alcoholic/addict. Making "amends" to persons you had harmed would be the task of the next pair of steps, 8 and 9. For 8, you list those persons, and ideally go over the list with your sponsor. For 9, you make "direct" amends to all those listed in ways that you had talked over with your sponsor and other members, and had learned about in Al-Anon meetings and literature.

Being able to make amends to others who weigh most heavily on your conscience should free you from deep-seated corrosive emotions. Learning how you might carry this out would call for a great deal of listening, talking, reading, and thought on your part. Merely one aspect of your amends to one person is briefly touched on here. That person is the alcoholic/addict in your life.

Amending or changing the way you relate to your alcoholic/

addict is a task you would have been working at from your start in Al-Anon. In steps 8 and 9, though, you would go at it with special intensity. Such intensity or focus often helps members achieve a degree of serenity toward the alcoholic/addict that goes beyond anything they felt before and that nothing ahead can disturb.

The ability to attain such a degree of serenity is sometimes described with the phrase "to detach with love." You could increasingly develop this ability as you progressed in the Al-Anon program and perhaps especially with steps 8 and 9.

Early in Al-Anon you see how you have become enmeshed emotionally in the turmoil of the life of the alcoholic/addict—worrying, pleading, blaming, hoping, fearing, raging, weeping, forgiving, hating. In time you understand that the turmoil, crises, and blowups result not from what the alcoholic/addict wants to do, but from what the disease forces him or her to do.

Your ability to detach may thus start when you can begin telling yourself, "That's not the person I know—that's the disease." You can detach the behavior caused by the disease from the person. "By seeing the person as separate from the disease, by detaching, we can stop being hurt by groundless insults or angered by outrageous lies," states a passage in *How Al-Anon Works for Families and Friends of Alcoholics*.[5] The book notes that you wouldn't blame or detest someone with a cold for sneezing. Instead, you'd feel some sympathy and draw back.

Later on, as you became better able to see how the disease erupts, you might find it helpful on occasion to detach physically as well as mentally. For instance, your alcoholic/addict may unconsciously need to provoke you to an argument so that your naturally enraged retorts justify storming out to drink or drug. At the very start of such a situation, you could detach by keeping silent and walking away. Or, in the face of seriously threatening, prolonged situations, you could move away.

• Reacting with Acceptance

In time, as your confidence and peace of mind and sense of self-worth grow in Al-Anon, you might come to view the alcoholic/addict with greater tolerance and charity. And in step 9, your amends to him or her could come in the form of consistently reacting in a new way of understanding and acceptance.

How this might come about is well put in the book *How Al-Anon Works for Families and Friends of Alcoholics*. "Our goal is to heal ourselves and our relationships with other human beings, not to coldly distance ourselves, especially from the people who matter most to us," it says. "In fact, detachment is far more compassionate and respectful than the unfeeling distancing or the compulsive involvement many of us have practiced in the past, for when we detach with love, we accept others exactly as they are."[6]

Three Al-Anon steps remain after step 9. In these, you would further your personal growth and recovery from the damage done by involvement with the alcoholic/addict. Step 10 reinforces the inventory-taking of step 4, while step 11 extends one's practice of spirituality in step 3. Step 12 primarily calls for the member to carry Al-Anon's message of recovery to others, thus safeguarding and improving that member's recovery.

[Will Your Al-Anon Efforts Lead to Recovery?]

Al-Anon and its members make no claim that the Al-Anon program will lead the alcoholic/addict in your life into recovery. "From the very beginning we learn that we are powerless to control an alcoholic's drinking," states *This Is Al-Anon*, an official pamphlet. "Until we stop trying to control, we will continue to live with the frustration that made us seek Al-Anon."[7]

However, even if you're not solving the addiction problem by joining Al-Anon, at least you're no longer unknowingly compounding the problem with your enabling and denial. In addition, the special motivating confrontation with the alcoholic/addict, called "intervention," which is described in chapter 2, quite often influences the alcoholic/addict to enter treatment and recovery. Your ongoing practice of the Al-Anon program may serve as a kind of low-pressure but constant intervention.

• What Al-Anon Does Promise

It is, of course, true that some substantial numbers of Al-Anon members do see the alcoholics/addicts in their lives actually begin recovery. No one has yet found if the proportion of those for whom this happens is higher than that in a comparable group of persons who never took part in Al-Anon. But even if the Al-Anon proportion were higher, you could still be disappointed in your individual case. No one can as yet predict why and when any one alcoholic/addict will begin recovery.

However, Al-Anon is able to make you a promise for which it has abundant proof. You'd hear that promise in the "Suggested Al-Anon/Alateen Welcome" statement that is read at the start of each meeting by many Al-Anon groups. "In Al-Anon we discover that no situation is really hopeless," runs the promise, "and that it is possible for us to find contentment and even happiness, whether the alcoholic is still drinking or not. . . ."[8]

[If the Alcoholic/Addict Starts Recovery]

One of the popular maxims that members of Al-Anon and AA pass along to one another advises: "Don't pray for an elephant unless you've got a big backyard." It just might happen that, after you've been in Al-Anon for some time, you may get the elephant you've prayed for. That is, your alcoholic/addict may actually start recovery.

If that should come about, you'd find that Al-Anon has outfitted you with a spacious and really wonderful backyard for this particular elephant. Family members and any others very close come under special strains when an alcoholic/addict begins recovery. These strains are in some cases so severe that they cause divorces or bitter breaks, or estrangements between parents and children. You'd learn about such cases, and reasons for them, in going to Al-Anon and Open AA Meetings.

Al-Anon functions at just about its best in providing means to navigate safely through such difficulties. It does so by helping family members adapt constructively to what in many ways are quite different lives for each of them in recovery. It can give you a recovery program you need in order to grow personally in harmony with the recovery of the alcoholic/addict you care about. And for you, this might be its most important benefit of all.

[*Four*]

The Work-Life Way: Programs to Start
Recovery for Employees or Professionals

Threats to their work—their livelihoods, jobs, professional licenses—can act as the most powerful force of all for moving some alcoholics/addicts into starting recovery. For them, work serves as their last fortress of denial. Losing their homes, their lovers, their kids, their health, their friends, their money, and their sanity won't even budge their addiction, so long as they can earn money.

"I'm absolutely all right because I can still work," these alcoholics/addicts tell themselves.

"Get off my back. I'm still bringing home the money," they roar at family members who say they might have a problem.

Doggedly trying to hang on to work may slow the remorseless march of addiction, in some cases. But in time, for the truly addicted, the disease always wins and any possibility of working ends.

How a Work Confrontation Can Jump-Start Recovery

Today, however, alcoholics/addicts stand perhaps a better chance than ever before of not having addiction ruin their working life. A great many companies and corporations today have developed employee assistance programs—called EAPs for short—that help alcoholics/addicts on their payrolls. And official bodies in such professions as medicine, dentistry, law, nursing, and pharmacy have introduced "impaired professional" or "assistance" programs that similarly help alcoholics/addicts in the profession.

You may be able to help the alcoholic/addict start on recovery through a program of this type. This is especially true if you are the employer or supervisor of the alcoholic/addict, or even just a fellow employee. It could also be true if you are his or her professional associate, partner, or superior.

Common to each type of program is a climax—a sort of shootout at the O.K. Corral. This is a confrontation with the alcoholic/addict by a person of authority. Ideally, impartial evidence of the problem will have been gathered with all due protection of the rights of the alcoholic/addict. He or she will be presented with it.

A choice of treatment and monitoring will be offered. Being fired or being stripped of professional certification will be the alternative. Often, understandably, the alcoholic/addict opts for recovery.

In these systems, the alcoholic/addict at least has a chance to change. Before EAP, no choice was offered. The person was simply gotten rid of.

Incidentally, these programs also deal with issues besides alcoholism/addiction. Overall, they are problems "including, but not limited to, health, marital, family, financial, alcohol, drug, legal, emotional, stress, or other personal issues that may affect job performance," according to the Employee Assistance Professionals Association.

Could You Spark an EAP Case for Your Alcoholic/Addict?

A natural thought for you is whether you might be able to get an EAP case started for the alcoholic/addict whom you'd like to help into recovery. This depends on your connection to her or him (and, of course, if he or she is an employee in an outfit having an EAP).

Your answer would be a resounding yes if you supervise the work of the alcoholic/addict. In fact, in your situation, an EAP action might be the most promising method at hand to influence the alcoholic/addict to accept treatment.

Moreover, starting an EAP case wouldn't be merely an option for you. It would very likely be a requirement of your job. Abuse of alcohol and other drugs by employees has been estimated to cost American businesses more than $100 billion a year.[1] Alcoholics/addicts generate these costs through abnormally high rates of accidents and injuries on (and off) the job, mistakes at work that can be costly or even fatal, sick days, absenteeism, and costs in healthcare benefits. In addition, alcoholics/addicts can endanger their fellow employees, make them do the work of the alcoholic/addict, and undermine morale.

• *In a Small Firm*

Your answer would also be yes if you're the owner of a small company and she or he is an employee. Your firm need not even have an established EAP program. Qualified EAP consultants operate in most parts of the country. You should be able to contract with one of them to plan an EAP program using outside services, and to provide them on an as-needed basis.

Your answer would be "yes, probably" if you're a fellow employee working closely with the alcoholic/addict. You might get an EAP case started by telling your supervisor in confidence the facts of incidents when the alcoholic/addict very badly failed to meet the needs of the job due to alcohol or drugs.

Your answer would be "probably not" if you're a close family member or friend outside the company where the alcoholic/addict works. However, you might exert some influence if you have happened to meet his or her supervisor or fellow workers socially, perhaps through friends or some company function for employee families.

In this case, you might get in touch with the supervisor or fellow worker and mention your worry over the alcoholic/addict. You could report facts of specific incidents in which the alcoholic/addict was incapacitated for work due to alcohol and/or drugs. The supervisor or fellow worker might then be able to add your facts to others documenting the need for EAP action.

There's a good chance that your alcoholic/addict works where there's an Employee Assistance Program. If you don't know whether there is, phone the Human Resources Department there to ask.

Many companies have adopted EAPs to lower costs. In addition, various federal requirements have led to still wider introduction of EAPs. The U.S. Department of Defense, the U.S. Department of Transportation, the U.S. Department of Energy, and the U.S. Nuclear Regulatory Commission require that workplaces they operate or regulate be free of abusers of alcohol or drugs.

• *Federal Agencies and Contractors*

All federal agencies, in fact, have been required to be drug-free workplaces since the signing of a Presidential Executive Order to that effect in 1986. Moreover, any business or other organization receiving more than $25,000 of the billions of dollars in federal contracts awarded annually comes under requirements of the Drug-Free Workplace Act. It became law in 1988.

These recipients of federal contracts (or grants, as for research) must have written policies that prohibit alcohol or drug abusers from affecting the workplace. They must also provide a program of alcoholism/addiction education for employees, among other requirements.

Not all features of an EAP are mandated by the act. But many contractors have found it advantageous to develop complete EAPs by adding the few remaining features.

• *For Employers, a Helpline*

Employers who have any questions about federal drug-free workplace requirements (including possibly required drug testing of employees), and about any aspect of EAPs, may obtain answers and information by phoning this toll-free "Workplace Helpline": 1-800-WORKPLACE (1-800-967-5752).

This Helpline is staffed Monday through Friday, 9 A.M. to

8 P.M. Eastern Time (U.S.). It is operated by the Center for Substance Abuse Prevention, U.S. Department of Health and Human Services.

What Would an EAP Case for Your Alcoholic/Addict Be Like?

Key to opening an EAP case for your alcoholic/addict would be the person gathering the facts that document repeated failures to fulfill the requirements of the job. This would most likely be the supervisor, or it could be an EAP specialist getting facts from the supervisor and others.

Many legal considerations would surround the process. Great care must be taken not to violate any of the rights of your alcoholic/addict—among them, rights to privacy, rights not to be subject to discrimination, rights not to be slandered, rights for equal employment opportunity, rights under federal statutes protecting those with disabilities, possibly rights as a labor union member.

Whoever builds the case must therefore be thoroughly trained, and must proceed with great care. What training is involved and what steps to take are set forth in full detail in the book *Turning Problem Employees into Successes: A Handbook for Managers and Supervisors*, by Carol Cox Smith (Minneapolis, Minn.: Johnson Institute, 1992).

No judgments are made and no conclusions are drawn by the case-compiler. Facts are recorded. They are backed up by evidence that's collected and by notes on statements by witnesses, much as for a case going to trial in court. "X staggered while walking and his speech was slurred" and "There was a strong smell of alcohol on X's breath" might be recorded (along with time and place and witness's name). A record would not note the conclusion "X was drunk," or even "X appeared to be drunk."

Confidentiality should be scrupulously maintained. Experts recommend that a code letter or number be used to identify the alcoholic/addict in the written records, rather than the employee's name. All the case records should be kept separately under lock and key, accessible only to the case-compiler.

Any fellow employee or other individual supplying facts is required to say nothing about the case or the facts supplied to anyone other than the case-compiler. During the building of the case, nothing whatever is said to the alcoholic/addict concerned. The case-compiler confers on the case only with a representative of the firm's EAP program designated for that purpose.

Thorough training of the supervisor assembling the case material on your alcoholic/addict would ideally prevent any enabling judgments by that supervisor. Enabling behavior of someone involved with an alcoholic/addict excuses or minimizes harm done by his or her addiction-driven actions.

The way that enabling develops in those living with an alcoholic/addict was described in chapter 3. Persons working with the alcoholic/addict can likewise become enablers. As such, they might dismiss accidents or arrests while drunk as just bad luck, or make up the work of the alcoholic/addict when he or she is out on a binge, or excuse many extra days out sick (ones actually caused by addiction) as instead due to involuntary health problems.

However, proper EAP training of the supervisor investigating your alcoholic/addict should put that supervisor on guard against any tendency to ignore or shade the truth and thus enable the addiction.

• When EAP Action Confronts Your Alcoholic/Addict

The evidence on your alcoholic/addict would document a great many of the incidents in which the employee failed in work performance and job responsibilities in ways obviously due to alcoholism/addiction (but with no mention whatever of alcoholism/ addiction as the cause). Then, typically, your alcoholic/addict would be called to a meeting with the supervisor who had compiled the case. The supervisor would be sympathetic and respectful, but firm. He or she would characterize the meeting as one called so that they could solve some problems together.

Those problems would be taken up in reviewing the facts and evidence of incidents of failure in job performance and responsibilities by your alcoholic/addict. Nothing would be said about alcohol or drug abuse. The supervisor would ask him or her to suggest how the resulting problems could be solved.

It's not uncommon for an alcoholic/addict to promise to improve when first confronted in this fashion. It's also not uncommon for the promise to be broken due to the addiction, resulting in new incidents of job failures. This leads to a second meeting for problem solving between the supervisor and the alcoholic/addict.

Whether in a first or a subsequent meeting, the supervisor would offer referral of the alcoholic/addict to an EAP counselor to work out a solution to the problems. This would be proposed sympathetically. If the alcoholic/addict refused the offer after some discussion, the supervisor would say that the alternative is to be let go (or, in some cases, to face some other penalizing action).

Work with the EAP counselor and other specialists the counselor might involve would lead to a diagnosis of alcoholism/ addiction. It would be accompanied by a recommendation for appropriate treatment with arrangements for leave and eventual return to the job. After completing treatment and returning to work, your alcoholic/addict would be subject to follow-ups for monitoring continued recovery.

You may recall from chapter 2 that close family members or friends sometimes join in an intervention meeting with the alcoholic/addict. That meeting is run to motivate her or him to start recovery by entering treatment.

As you can see, an EAP case involving your alcoholic/addict resembles that kind of intervention, though it would be narrower in scope than an intervention brought by family and friends. But it could have greater effect on some alcoholics/addicts because of its basic focus on the security and confidence their earning powers bring.

Some individuals whose drinking or drugging at times causes serious harm and failures may not have developed the disease of addiction. Professionals in the field call persons like these "substance abusers." Addicts, by contrast, are termed "chemically dependent."

Substance abusers may or may not become addicts. Some alcoholics/addicts in recovery can recall a number of years in which drinking caused few problems in their lives. But, looking back, they realize that at some point, in a striking phrase they sometimes use, they "crossed the line." On the far side of that line, they drank when they didn't want to. They couldn't stop drinking once they had started. Needing to drink came before anything else in their lives. They had become addicts.

Others in recovery tell of a different experience. From the very first time they drank or took drugs and got high, getting high again became one of the most important things in their lives. From the start, they were addicts.

However, it may be that the person whose drinking or drugging concerns you is a substance abuser rather than an addict. He or she may still fail in job responsibilities because of drinking or drugging often enough to bring on an EAP case. If so, the result should still be beneficial. The EAP confrontation and consequent counseling or treatment might prevent her or him from continuing on into addiction.

• *Random Drug-Testing at Work*

Your alcoholic/addict might also be moved to start on recovery where he or she works by random testing for drugs. Many companies with functions greatly affecting the public safety have programs in which employees must undergo drug-testing.

Chief among these are public transportation firms and agencies. Since 1989 the U.S. Department of Transportation (DOT) has required that employees holding "safety sensitive" jobs be tested for drug or alcohol use. Among these are the employees of airlines, mass transit lines, railroads, trucking firms, and companies with ships for passengers or freight.

Some other types of companies, like public utilities generating electrical power, also often tend to have drug-testing programs for employees. Such testing appears to be in especially wide use for employees in nuclear power plants.

In addition, many employers of other types have started random drug-testing of their employees. They have done so in response to financial incentives offered by the federal government. Those incentives are provided to induce any employer to join in the federal drug-free workplace program voluntarily.

In being tested, the alcoholic/addict would typically be asked to provide a urine sample, which would be collected, identified, and sent to a laboratory for analysis. This would be carried out in much the same way it is dealt with in a doctor's office visit.

Your alcoholic/addict would be more likely to face such testing for drugs or alcohol in applying for a job than in the course of holding a job. Employers with drug-testing programs more often test all new job applicants, while testing only random samples of their employees.

Random testing programs are designed to have a preventive effect, for the most part. For example, if your alcoholic/addict worked for a firm under DOT drug-testing regulations, he or she would face possible testing only once a year. Also, only a portion of a company's employees are required to be tested in any one year. For the year 2000, for instance, those portions were as follows: For truck drivers and mass transit operators: 50 percent test rate for drugs, 10 percent rate for alcohol. For airline and railroad employees: 25 percent test rate for drugs, 10 percent rate for alcohol.

So, if your alcoholic/addict were a truck driver, only 50 percent of all the firm's truck drivers would need to be tested in the year. And the 50 percent set to be tested would be selected with the use of a mathematical "random number generator" (one run by a computer).

As a result, your truck driver alcoholic/addict might be tested for drugs two or three years in a row, or might go for two or three years without being tested. But the chance of being tested would always be there.

Coming up positive on a test would bring on much the same actions as an EAP case. Your alcoholic/addict would be informed of the results and referred to a counselor for professional diagnosis and, probably, appropriate treatment.

Hair is also tested for drug use in a few instances, and the police widely test the breath for blood-alcohol content. Analysis of even one hair can reveal more about past use of drugs (cocaine particularly) than a urine test. Blood-alcohol content of 0.1 percent or higher is defined as the concentration sufficient for a charge of Driving While Intoxicated (DWI) almost universally in the United States.

Much controversy surrounds random drug testing, not only testing of employees but of athletes and of students. However, many millions of employees are subject to it today. And it could help lead the alcoholic/addict who worries you into recovery.

For Your Doctor or Lawyer Alcoholic/Addict, the Profession's Way Out

Is your alcoholic/addict a physician, dentist, nurse, pharmacist, or other licensed health-care professional? A lawyer? An airline pilot? If so, her or his profession has developed special programs and procedures for getting alcoholics/addicts into recovery.

An alcoholic/addict worrying you could be protected by two special features of these programs. One is that the programs keep the addicted individual's identity completely confidential. Indeed, almost nothing about the programs themselves is ever disclosed beyond the inner circles of the profession and its government regulating bodies.

In the second protective feature, the programs would provide means by which your alcoholic/addict could continue being licensed (or otherwise credentialed) to practice as a professional. However, continuing to be licensed would require that your alcoholic/addict go through treatment and aftercare as directed, and continue to be monitored for ongoing abstinence.

• Recovery for the Doctor
Fellow practitioners would be the most likely persons to trigger the steps leading your alcoholic/addict doctor toward recovery. "Phy-

sicians have an ethical obligation to report impaired, incompetent, and unethical colleagues," declares a recent resolution of the American Medical Association (Resolution 9[A-99] of the AMA's House of Delegates).

Such impairment should be reported to the "in-house impairment program" of the hospital with which the doctor is associated, the resolution adds. If that can't be done, the report should go to an "external impaired physician program." External programs of this kind "typically would be operated by the local medical societies or state licensing boards."

You might want to inquire about a possible impaired physician program for the alcoholic/addict worrying you. If so, you would inquire with one of these three sources—the hospital with which he or she is associated, your state or county medical society, or the board in the state government that licenses physicians.

As an example of an external program, the Medical Society of the State of New York has provided a way for a physician impaired by alcoholism/addiction to avoid being referred to state officials for possible license revocation. Instead, if no patient has been harmed, and the doctor agrees to accept treatment and rehabilitation, he or she comes under the supervision of the Committee for Physician's Health. This is a body of the Medical Society of the state.

If the physician happened to be your alcoholic/addict, he or she would then be able to have his or her license become inactive temporarily—and confidentially. Later, your alcoholic/addict would have the chance to apply to have the license reactivated, after proving to be fully restored to competence for practice.

Typical Program Takes at Least Four Months and Two Years to Complete:
The kind of treatment and aftercare program your alcoholic/addict

doctor might go into has been outlined by a specialized treatment center, the Ridgeview Institute in Smyrna, Georgia. It commented that most patients in its specialized health-care professionals program are M.D.s, R.N.s, D.D.s., and pharmacists. Of the program, it summarizes:

> Minimum stay, 4 months. Phase I, 29-day inpatient treatment. Phase II, 30-day outpatient day program with residence and activities in halfway house system. Phase III, "mirror-imaging phase," 2-month assignment to one of the 21 Atlanta metropolitan area Alcohol and Drug Treatment Centers counseling other alcoholics/addicts in their first few days of recovery. Follow-up for minimum of 2 years by the impaired professionals programs in the various states.[2]

Among other treatment facilities offering programs for health-care professionals are Timberlawn Psychiatric Hospital in Dallas, Texas; Brighton Hospital in Brighton, Michigan; and the Hazelden Foundation in Center City, Minnesota.

While in treatment, your alcoholic/addict doctor is likely to learn of special groups in Alcoholics Anonymous consisting only of doctors and other health-care professionals. They help others in their professions enter and stay in recovery. They meet separately, in large part, in order to be able to share their addicted experiences only with like professionals.

Your alcoholic/addict might find one such group quite remarkable, the International Doctors in Alcoholics Anonymous, IDAA. It dates from 1949, and is now "an organization of over 6,000 physicians, dentists, veterinarians, and other doctoral level health-care professionals who have found recovery from addiction" (according to its Internet site on the World Wide Web). It holds regional meetings both in and outside the United States.

As of this writing, your alcoholic/addict doctor could reach the IDAA as follows:

IDAA
P.O. Box 199
Augusta, MO 63332
Phone: 636-482-4548
Fax: 632-228-4102
Web site: http://members.aol.com/aadocs

• *State Association Programs for Alcoholic/Addict Nurses*

It may be that the alcoholic/addict you want to help is a nurse. If so, for general backing, the American Nurses Association by policy maintains that nurses who are chemically dependent should be given the option of treatment and rehabilitation before license withdrawal.

However, it is the nurse associations for the individual states of the United States that provide programs putting this policy into practice. An alcoholic/addict nurse of yours would accordingly most often find help in starting recovery from his or her state nurses association. Your nurse could request or be referred for such help without risking her or his state nursing license.

Many of the state nursing associations have active programs to help alcoholic/addict nurses. "Peer Assistance Program" is generally used as the name, as, for instance, with the Ohio and Rhode Island state association programs. Georgia's association, though, uses "Nurse Advocacy Program," while the New York association terms its program "Statewide Peer Assistance for Nurses."

Intervention for the Alcoholic/Addict Nurse: Your alcoholic/addict nurse would be most likely to be referred to one of these peer assistance programs by a fellow nurse or supervisor. One frequent function of the programs is to conduct interventions to motivate a nurse to accept treatment. Or, if you instead did not work with the nurse but were a family member or friend, you could contact the state association program in the nurse's behalf.

You might contact the state association program to obtain information or to offer facts about incidents involving work that may evidence addiction. If your state association does not happen to have a nurse assistance program, you might ask the office of such a program for a neighboring state for information and other sources of help.

You could find out how to reach your state's nurses association by a phone or letter request to the American Nurses Association, as follows—

American Nurses Association
600 Maryland Avenue, S.W.
Washington, DC 20024-2571
Phone (toll-free) 1-800-274-4ANA (1-800-274-4262)

Or, via the World Wide Web, links connect you directly to the home pages of the state nurses associations at this Web site: http://www.ana.org/snaweb.htm.

A slightly different Web site gives you the addresses and phone numbers of the state nurses association offices. That site is: http://www.ana.org/snaaddr.htm.

Two additional types of help might be turned to for help with alcoholic/addict nurses. One is an Employee Assistance Program where he or she works. A number of hospitals have EAPs, which have essentially the same functions as the EAPs offered by a great many employers of all varieties.

Self-help twelve-step groups especially for nurses (or nurses and other health-care professionals) represent the second type of possible help. Personal inquiries in AA or Al-Anon circles might discover such groups. One such organization is patterned after International Doctors in AA. It is International Nurses Anonymous, INA. Its mailing address, phone number, and Web site are:

International Nurses Anonymous
1020 Sunset Drive
Lawrence, KS 66044
Phone: 913-842-3893
Web site: http://www.crml.uab.edu/~jah/ina.html

• *The Lawyer Alcoholic/Addict*
An alcoholic/addict who worries you could find much help from peers in the profession if he or she happens to be a lawyer. Many leaders in the profession have been active in setting up "lawyer assistance programs," or LAPs.

For alcoholic/addict lawyers, "these programs employ the use of intervention, peer counseling, and referral to twelve-step programs to assist in the lawyer's recovery process," notes a report of the American Bar Association. It adds that attorneys may have special need for such help, stating: ". . . while ten percent of the general population has problems with alcohol abuse, anywhere from fifteen to eighteen percent of the lawyer population battles the same problem."[3]

Alcoholic/addict lawyers like yours would find such LAPs in all fifty states of the United States today, largely due to the work of the Commission on Lawyer Assistance Programs of the American Bar Association. It works to get such programs started and assist with their development and coordination.

How an alcoholic/addict lawyer like yours might be helped by such programs would vary from state to state. Some states have staff administrators who are recovering alcoholics/addicts. Informing lawyers within their areas about their program is a function they carry out by visits to larger firms, conference talks, and mailings.

Also, on occasion, these administrators do direct case work. "Not long ago, for example, a judge in one rural district got drunk, abandoned his family, and went to live with his girlfriend in a trailer park," a lawyer noted in a recent article. "The director of the state's assistance program drove out and fetched him."[4]

Were your alcoholic/addict lawyer in Ohio, she or he would take a course in addiction required by the state for Continuing Legal Education—a requirement instigated by the state's LAP backers. One estimate credits all efforts by those Ohio backers with generating recovery from alcoholism/addiction for some two dozen judges and six hundred lawyers.

Or, if your alcoholic/addict lawyer were in Oregon, she or he would have to pay into an attorney malpractice insurance fund—one similarly resulting from work by LAP adherents. The greater the number of malpractice insurance losses due to alcoholism/addiction of attorneys, the higher the levies paid by all other Oregon attorneys. This gives them all a direct financial incentive to help malpracticing and addicted colleagues start on recovery.[5]

No Risk of Disbarment or Disgrace: An alcoholic/addict lawyer of yours could benefit from one enormously important achievement of LAPs in the profession. By admitting addiction and accepting treatment and monitoring, he or she would not risk disbarment and loss of authorization to practice. Nor would starting on recovery be likely to risk loss of a job, if he or she were employed by a law firm.

Moreover, the fact that your alcoholic/addict sought help through an LAP would be kept completely confidential. He or she would thus be protected against any risk of disgrace in the profession.

Various self-help groups of formerly addicted lawyers that have been formed also directly help addicted lawyers start recovery, while also safeguarding continued recovery for their members. Notable among these is "The Other Bar," a loose coalition of AA groups especially for attorneys that has thousands of members. Notable also is the similar "International Lawyers in Alcoholics Anonymous," ILAA, inspired by the International Doctors of AA.

You can obtain information about LAPs for a possible alcoholic/addict lawyer you know by contacting the ABA, as follows:

Commission on Lawyer Assistance Programs
American Bar Association
541 N. Fairbanks Court
Chicago, IL 60611
Phone: 312-988-5522
Web site: http://www.abanet.org/cpr/colap/home.html

• Alcoholic/Addict Pilots

You will, of course, feel a special sense of urgency if the alcoholic/addict you want to help is an airplane pilot. So would many others associated with the pilot. Similar feelings of urgency by pilots themselves and the airlines that employ them have led to especially stringent and comprehensive programs for alcoholic/addict pilots.

Jointly responsible for these programs are the Air Line Pilots Association (ALPA) and the airlines (through the EAPs of the individual firms). ALPA is the pilots' labor union, affiliated with the AFL-CIO. Also involved in the programs is the Office of Aviation Medicine of the Federal Aviation Administration (FAA).

Before the 1970s, evidence of alcoholism/addiction in a commercial airline pilot often led to swift cancellation of the pilot's license by the FAA. Today, however, an alcoholic/addict pilot is able to retain his or her license contingent on going through a demanding program of treatment, rehabilitation, and aftercare.

Pilots are led to enter their special programs in a variety of ways, one of which might correspond to your situation. One study's findings of the ways in which commercial airline pilots began treatment were as follows:

- 23 percent began treatment on their own initiative.
- 60 percent were sent to treatment by the ALPA, their airline, or both.
- 17 percent entered treatment because of their families, their counselors, or law courts.[6]

Should you want to refer your alcoholic/addict airline pilot for treatment, or inquire about it, you can use directory assistance to call the Employee Assistance Program at the main offices of the airline for which the pilot works. Or you can reach the ALPA as follows:

Human Resources Department
Air Line Pilots Association
P.O. Box 1169
Herndon, VA 20172
Fax: 703-464-2110
E-mail: humanresources@alpa.org

[**Religious Vocations**]

It's possible that the alcoholic/addict in your life is a minister, priest, pastor, rabbi, monk, nun, or other professional following a religious vocation. Some men and women in religious life do develop addictions.

Most often, those who do are cared for by official agencies of their religion. These are much the same agencies that would intervene in behalf of the alcoholics/addicts if they were stricken instead by a physical illness or a psychological breakdown.

Such agencies are typically empowered to order the individual into treatment. The agencies tend to take such action quietly, with least possible public awareness, in order to avoid embarrassment or disruption.

In some cases, help comes from individuals from their congregations, or from friends or relatives. Accordingly, should you want to help an alcoholic/addict who is in a religious vocation, you might first proceed as with any other individual. That is, by getting the person to start recovery through means such as AA, Al-Anon, a professional intervention, or a counseling technique. The alternative would be to report your concerns and ask for help for the person from higher officials in the religious faith.

[*Five*]

The Law-Enforcement Way: Drunk-Driving Arrests, Drug Courts, Prison Programs

G *etting arrested and* jailed might lie ahead for an alcoholic/addict you care about if he or she continues to abuse alcohol or drugs. Most probable is an arrest for Driving Under the Influence (DUI) of alcohol or drugs (which includes Driving While Intoxicated, DWI). Next most likely would be an arrest for drug possession.

But alcoholics/addicts frenzied by their addictions also get arrested for various other offenses. Among them, theft (for stealing to support their habits), dealing drugs, assault (for street fights or bar fights when affronted), and, sadly, domestic violence.

Addicts get arrested for almost any and all crimes, in fact. Studies have shown that as many as four out of every five criminals in American prisons have serious problems with alcoholism/addiction.[1]

Being arrested, taken to a police station, and perhaps locked up in a jail cell would, of course, be bitter experiences for the alcoholic/addict you're worried about. However, just such experiences are often the events that finally impel a number of alcoholics/addicts to begin recovery.

142

Your alcoholic/addict might be so impelled in various ways— the most direct of which would be if arrest and even jailing are shocking enough in themselves to break through the wall of denial. Your alcoholic/addict would then resolve to accept treatment or become deadly serious about trying AA.

You (and perhaps others close to the alcoholic/addict) might help with that resolve in three very important ways: First, by not enabling the alcoholic/addict through shielding him or her from the consequences of the drunken/drugged actions leading to the arrest. Second, by supporting his or her resolve with great enthusiasm. Third, by having on hand complete information on where and how to start in treatment, AA meetings, or both.

However, if such a shock were not enough, further law-enforcement actions might be taken to impel your alcoholic/addict toward recovery in other ways. Among them are:

- Probation under "correctional supervision" that requires entering treatment or attending AA meetings. Your alcoholic/addict might be granted this conditionally by the court, in place of imprisonment, if he or she has received a DUI or DWI conviction.
- Mandated treatment and long supervision in place of imprisonment, in a nationwide special program, either the Drug Courts Program or the Treatment Alternatives to Street Crime (TASC) program. Your alcoholic/addict might accept treatment instead of prison in either of these "diversion" programs if he or she had been arrested as a nonviolent offender whose crime had been due mainly to drug addiction.
- Treatment for alcoholism/addiction in prison. Your alcoholic/

addict might get treatment in one of the relatively few treatment programs in federal and state prisons.

Jail Terms of Six Months or More for Drunk Driving

Your alcoholic/addict stands the largest chances of having the law threaten her or his addiction because of driving. In each current year, about one in every 125 licensed drivers in the United States is arrested for driving under the influence of alcohol or drugs—in all, about 1,400,000 people. (Such arrests and prosecutions alone cost the country more than $5 billion a year.)

Death is also most likely to involve driving for your alcoholic/addict. Almost four out of every ten traffic fatalities in the United States involve alcohol. And your alcoholic/addict need not even be driving in order to die. Some three out of every ten pedestrians killed by cars are intoxicated.

Small wonder, then, that a first-time DWI conviction could result in a six-month jail sentence for your alcoholic/addict. That's the median sentence, according to Mothers Against Drunk Driving (MADD), which is the source for the other statistics. MADD is a nonprofit organization campaigning to end drunk driving—and especially the killing of children by drunk drivers—in the United States.

• Breath and Urine Tests Might Convict the Alcoholic/Addict

Conviction of your alcoholic/addict on a DUI charge would probably be based on a test of either breath or urine. Such a test would result if your alcoholic/addict were stopped by police for erratic driving reflecting dangerous incapability, or if stopped on the road at one of the sobriety checkpoints that have become increasingly common in recent years.

If thus stopped, your alcoholic/addict would probably be asked by the police to blow into a portable device called a Breathalyzer. It would produce evidence of his or her blood alcohol content, BAC. A BAC of one-tenth of 1 percent (or more) alcohol in the blood—0.10 percent—would be evidence sufficient for a conviction throughout the United States.

More than seventeen states and the District of Columbia had set the level for DWI conviction at 0.08 percent or more BAC by 1999—lower than the 0.10 percent limit. Studies show that reducing the limit to this 0.08 percent substantially reduces traffice fatalities, injuries, and related costs. As a result, the federal government has mounted a program to encourage all states to adopt the 0.08 percent limit.

If your alcoholic/addict were a 180-pound man, he would reach that 0.10 percent BAC by having some five drinks in two hours (with a drink defined as 1.5 ounces of liquor or 12 ounces of beer). However, if your alcoholic/addict instead were a 100-pound woman, she would reach the 0.10 percent BAC with only about three drinks in two hours.

When Alcohol Alone Can Kill: And, by the way, just three or four times those amounts would probably put your alcoholic/addict into a coma, with an 0.30 percent to 0.40 percent BAC. Six times those amounts would almost certainly kill. Each year, it seems, some college students die in just this way in fraternity hazing for new pledges. Death results when alcohol sufficiently suppresses heartbeat and breathing.

For drug testing, the police would have your alcoholic/addict go with them to the police station, and would request a urine sample. Testing of the sample would provide evidence of the identities and amounts of the drugs and alcohol your alcoholic/addict had taken.

[Jail or Recovery?]

Getting a first DWI conviction would risk driving-license suspension as well as jail for the alcoholic/addict. But it would also be fairly likely to mean a chance at starting recovery instead of some months in jail.

Courts widely offer probation instead of prison to drivers convicted on a DWI charge. That probation is offered on the condition that the alcoholic/addict accepts alcoholism/addiction treatment or regular AA attendance or both. Regular meetings with a probation officer are required for the alcoholic/addict. In these meetings, the alcoholic/addict on probation provides evidence of attendance at treatment sessions and/or AA meetings. Urine testing to prove continued abstinence can also be required.

Some nine out of every ten persons with DWI convictions were granted probation over imprisonment in the 1990s. Your alcoholic/addict would accordingly have a substantial chance of getting probation after a possible DWI. However, those chances would drop sharply for later DWI convictions. Fewer than one in five DWIs got probation after a second DWI. After a third DWI, that proportion dropped to fewer than one in every sixteen.[2]

As these figures for second and third DWI convictions reflect, probation contingent on going for treatment and/or AA meetings does not necessarily result in lasting recovery. This is also borne out by personal accounts of results from group DWI programs at treatment centers and AA meetings with DWI-mandated attendees.

Some alcoholics/addicts forced by these court orders into treatment or AA do make it into continued recovery, however. Of course, your alcoholic/addict would be fortunate if this proved true in his or her case. If not, at least he or she will have been exposed to a taste of recovery that could become pivotal when the addiction makes life worse.

For the Hard-Core Addict, a Drug Court Would Go Far

Especially effective court action to help an alcoholic/addict not only try recovery but also make recovery go on working could be in store for the alcoholic/addict who concerns you, on two conditions. One is that he or she has been arrested on a nonviolent felony drug charge, and has a history of severe drug addiction. The other is that he or she comes by chance before one of some 350 or more special "drug courts" operating across the United States (or a similar court, in the TASC program or in a special state program, as explained later).

In one of these drug courts, your addict could be sent right after arrest not to jail but into an intensive outpatient treatment program. In it, he or she would attend sessions as often as every day, getting group therapy, individual counseling, and alcoholism/addiction education. Frequent urine tests would be required to verify abstinence. The addict would have required status hearings with the drug court's judge every one or two weeks.

But such treatment for a specified number of months would be only the beginning for your addict. Drug courts commonly also require addicts to:

- earn a high-school equivalency diploma (if they don't have one); get and hold a job;
- be financially responsible—in ways that include paying current bills (including ones for drug court charges) and keeping current on child-support payments, if any; and
- get a sponsor, who would most often be a sponsor in AA (or another twelve-step recovery support group like NA or CA).

Some drug courts would also require the addict to put in a number of community service hours, as compensation in kind for the services provided in the drug court program.

Still other rehabilitation services would typically be given to your addict through the drug court program. Among these might be medical care, vocational and family counseling, and educational guidance.

"A fundamental premise of the drug-court approach is that cessation of drug abuse requires not only well-structured treatment services," a recent report notes, "but coordinated and comprehensive programs of other rehabilitation services to address the underlying personal problems of the drug user, and promote his or her long-term reentry into society."[3]

Your addict should have substantial chances for continuing on to stable recovery through a drug court program. A comparatively high rate of 70 percent or more of the addicts going all the way through "graduate" into clean and sober lives. Among such graduates, the re-arrest rate for drug offenses is less than 4 percent.

You and your addict could thank the Dade County Circuit Court in Miami, Florida, for getting the drug courts programs started. In 1989, that Florida court introduced the first drug court. It sought to replace costly revolving-door crime and imprisonment of drug addicts with treatment and rehabilitation. Its success led to introduction of the Drug Courts Program of the U.S. Department of Justice in 1994.

By mid-1999, more than 140,000 addicts had been enrolled in more than 350 drug court programs, according to then U.S. Attorney General Janet Reno. Such programs have been introduced or considered in all fifty states, she noted. The Justice Department's Drug Courts Program helps fund drug courts, which are started by local judicial authorities or individual states.[4]

A kind of forerunner and parallel to the drug court programs might involve an addict of yours in some twenty-seven states. Begun in 1972, this is an intervention program for hard-core addicts arrested for drug offenses (usually drug possession, but often drug-dealing). It is called Treatment Alternatives to Street Crime, TASC.

As with drug courts, TASC diverts addicts from imprisonment into court-supervised treatment. TASC courts are begun and operated by local or state judicial bodies.

Voters in Arizona are responsible for a home-grown variant of the drug-court approach that might involve an addict of yours in that state. Called the Drug Treatment and Education Fund, the program was approved by 57 percent of the voters. Their action came in a 1998 referendum on Proposition 200, the Drug Medicalization, Prevention, and Control Act.

Ironically, should your addict happen to benefit from the Arizona program, funding for his or her treatment would come in part from a tax on liquor sales.

Savings of $34 per Addict per Day, Totaling $2,500,000 per Year: Not
only would your addict fare better in mandated treatment than in
prison through the Arizona program, but also his or her treatment
services would cost the state only $16.06 a day, as against $50 a day
to keep him or her in prison, according to an Arizona Supreme
Court report on the program. That $16.06 covers the cost of in-
tensive drug treatment, counseling, and frequent urine testing to
guarantee abstinence.

Those savings in all totaled more than $2,500,000 in the pro-
gram's first fiscal year. Still larger savings were expected over time.

More than three-quarters of the addicts in the program consistently test drug-free. Addicts who don't, or who otherwise refuse
to comply, are dropped from the program. "When we can't get
someone to change, we send them to prison," says Barbara Brod-
erick, state director of adult probation.

Arizona claims that the program makes it the first state to man-
date treatment for all nonviolent drug offenders instead of putting
them in prison. Judge Rudy Gerber of the Arizona Court of Ap-
peals has said the program takes a public health approach, and improves on the former "revolving door experience of drug offenders."

For your alcoholic/addict, being in the Arizona program would
have one drawback over his or her participation in a typical drug
court program. In these, the alcoholic/addict would be able to go
into treatment as an alternative to trial and conviction and a criminal record. But the Arizona program would first convict the al-
coholic/addict and only then provide treatment.[5]

***Possibly High Future Drug-Court Chances for Your Alcoholic/Addict in
California or New York:*** As of 2001, your alcoholic/addict would

also face possibly high future chances of having a drug court route her or him into treatment instead of jail in the states of California or New York. Recent actions in these states assured or promised large expansions in their drug-court programs that shift addicts due for convictions for nonviolent crimes from jail to supervised treatment.

Your alcoholic/addict might benefit most immediately from such action in the case of California. If convicted there of possessing (for personal use) or using illegal drugs, he or she would be required to receive probation and drug treatment instead of imprisonment. This would result from approval by a whopping 61 percent majority referendum vote for California's Proposition 36 in the November 2000 elections. It requires that most persons so convicted receive probation and treatment if they are first or second offenders. It is projected overall to reduce the number of California prison inmates by some 36,000 a year, with net savings of some $16,000 a year per inmate (totaling $560,000,000 a year).[6]

In New York State, your alcoholic/addict might face higher drug-court chances through two recent actions. State Chief Judge Judith S. Kaye took the first of the actions in mid-2000. She ordered all New York courts to start phasing in a program that could have your alcoholic/addict diverted from imprisonment for a nonviolent crime into drug treatment.

In this program, your alcoholic/addict would be offered such drug treatment if he or she were charged with a nonviolent crime like robbery or prostitution, tested positive for drugs, and pleaded guilty. If he or she did not accept such treatment, or entered it and had a relapse, your alcoholic/addict would be sentenced to jail. Treatment for him or her would typically run two years, and would include ongoing drug tests and court monitoring.

As many as ten thousand addicted criminals a year will be diverted into drug treatment instead of prison by the program, according to Judge Kaye. She estimated that the program would save the state some $500 million a year in costs for prisons and social services when fully operational in 2003. However, your alcoholic/addict would not be eligible for this drug-court program if convicted under the state's Rockefeller-era laws on drug possession and trafficking.[7]

New York State's second action that might heighten future drug-court chances for your alcoholic/addict was taken by Governor George E. Pataki in early 2001. He proposed that the legislature enact changes in rigid drug laws adopted in the Governor Rockefeller era of the 1970s. If adopted, those changes would enable judges to offer mandatory treatment instead of prison in some cases. They would also provide for lesser sentences and more discretion by judges in sentencing. Current laws that Pataki proposed changing include a provision under which a judge would be required to impose a sentence of imprisonment for fifteen years to life on your alcoholic/addict if he or she were convicted of possession of more than four ounces of cocaine or heroin, or for selling two or more ounces of either.[8]

In Prison, Some but Often All Too Scarce Treatment for Your Alcoholic/Addict

Should the alcoholic/addict who concerns you somehow be sent to a federal or state prison, there is still some chance that he or she could begin treatment and recovery there. Alcohol and drugs play such a huge part in crime that prison authorities have had almost no choice but to introduce alcoholism/addiction treatment programs for inmates.

One great irony in the current situation, however, might affect your alcoholic/addict in prison. In recent years, the number of persons imprisoned for drug-related convictions has grown enormously. But over the same time, treatment for inmates has not been increased anywhere near as rapidly.

How large a part alcohol and drugs play in crime—and in increasing the risk of prison for an alcoholic/addict worrying you—can be seen in arrest records of prison inmates. Among those in state prisons for violent crimes in one recent year, more than four out of every ten had been under the influence of alcohol when committing their crimes. Three out of every ten had been high on drugs when committing their violent crimes.

Drugs have also played an immense role in the explosive growth of prisons in recent years. You can see this in the fact that the prison population has tripled in the decades since 1980—to more than 1,800,000 inmates. And an alcoholic/addict in prison today has lots of company. Some 60 percent of all federal prison inmates have been convicted on drug charges, as have 22 percent of all inmates in state prisons.[9]

But even with all the fellow alcoholics/addicts in prison, your alcoholic/addict would have less chance of treatment now than in past years. The percentages of inmates receiving mandated drug treatment fell substantially from 1991 to 1997—in federal prisons, from 15.7 percent to 9.2 percent, and in state prisons from 24.5 percent to 9.7 percent.[10]

Another sad irony would apply to the case of your alcoholic/

addict should he or she be imprisoned for drug possession or dealing due to addiction. As the Arizona taxpayers learned, your alcoholic/addict could be given intensive treatment and rehabilitation at a cost only one-third the price of keeping him or her in prison.

• Treatment in Prison

An alcoholic/addict of yours in prison would be fortunate indeed if he or she happened to be put in a treatment program of the "therapeutic community" type. Only relatively few prisons offer such programs for inmates. Those that do have achieved impressive rates of recovery.

Your alcoholic/addict would be far more likely to have a chance, if he or she wanted, to take part in a limited treatment program. In some prisons, a chance like this is offered through one or more substance abuse counselors on the prison staff. Your alcoholic/addict might typically have the option of going once a week to a group discussion or therapy session run by the counselor.

Also, at quite a few prisons, AA members volunteer to hold regular AA meetings monthly or more often in the prison for interested inmates. NA and CA members also run volunteer meetings in prisons.

Some few inmates begin stable recovery after receiving such help from staff counselors or from volunteers who are themselves recovering alcoholics/addicts, but they seem to be those men and women who spontaneously "hit bottom" yet still have some hope.

Key-Crest Program in Delaware Works in Prison: An alcoholic/addict of yours in prison would be most likely to succeed in recovery if he or she entered a special treatment program in the Delaware state prison system (or a very similar program elsewhere). Key-Crest is the Delaware program's name. Actually, Key-Crest is a potent combination of three interconnected programs, called phases.

Key and Crest (phases I and II) represent treatment of the type generally termed therapeutic community. Chapter 6 covers this type of treatment for alcoholism/addiction in some detail. Briefly, if your alcoholic/addict entered a therapeutic-community treatment program, he or she would start living for as long as six months or a year in the program's quarters with the other patients. He or she would be subject to a strict and rigorous daily regimen designed to change basic patterns of behavior and thinking.

In Key-Crest, your alcoholic/addict would spend twelve months in Key, phase I, living in a therapeutic community in prison separate from the other inmates. He or she would then move into the Crest Outreach Center, phase II, for six months. Crest is a therapeutic community serving as a work-release facility. In it, your alcoholic/addict would work outside the prison.

Aftercare makes up phase III of Key-Crest. As part of this phase, your alcoholic/addict would have been given a supervised release from prison, such as parole. He or she would be required to spend six more months in aftercare, which would include continued counseling and group therapy.

Your alcoholic/addict would be very likely to make it into stable recovery if he or she were to go all the way through the Key-Crest program. Studies have found that, among those completing it, 76 percent of them are drug-free eighteen months after being released from prison.[11]

And should your alcoholic/addict happen to be sent to prison in Delaware, he or she would be almost certain to go into the program. Delaware requires "every inmate with a sentence of a year or more" to enter Key-Crest.[12]

New York's Pioneer Program: If your alcoholic/addict were to be in-carcerated instead in New York State, he or she might enter the program that inspired Key-Crest and similar programs across the United States. Its goal is stated in the program's name: Stay'n Out.

Called "the ground-breaking prison-based TC [therapeutic community] after which . . . other prison TCs around the country were modeled," Stay'n Out is also said to have been "first established by recovered addicts who also were ex-offenders."[13]

Your alcoholic/addict would optimally spend some nine to twelve months in a Stay'n Out therapeutic-community program. It operates units for men or for women inmates only in selected state prisons in New York.

Prison Programs in Other States: In all, more than one hundred therapeutic-community programs operate in federal and state pris-ons. Others that seem to be especially well-known are:

- Amity, in California
- Cornersteone, in Oregon
- Kyle New Vision, in Texas

Any of these therapeutic-community programs in prisons might prove unusually helpful in getting an alcoholic/addict of yours started in recovery. "Research shows that such TCs are effective with diverse locales and populations," one authority observes. "In-deed, recent studies consistently demonstrate that a substantial pro-portion of even the most intransigent hard-core offenders can be helped to change while in custody."[14]

[Six]

The Therapeutic-Community Way: Daytop, Phoenix House, Samaritan, Others

If *the alcoholic/addict* who has you worried seems severely addicted to drugs especially, he or she might need the therapeutic-community type of treatment in order to get successfully started on recovery. Your alcoholic/addict might also be right for a therapeutic community if he or she can't function at all in daily life—in ways like making a living, being responsible with close friends and family members, taking care of self and clothes and living quarters, and, particularly, obeying the laws.

Should your alcoholic/addict also be a teenager, therapeutic-community treatment might best help the youngster. Homeless or runaway teenagers who've gotten hooked on drugs enter therapeutic-community treatment in fairly large numbers—as do rebellious addicted teenagers from outwardly comfortable homes. Therapeutic-community programs for adolescents include schooling as well as treatment.

However, you and your alcoholic/addict need not decide in the abstract whether a therapeutic community might provide especially effective treatment. As its first stage, such treatment typically begins with a detailed assessment of an applicant. Whether your alcoholic/

addict would be appropriate for such treatment would be evaluated in the first interviews of assessment.

How badly your alcoholic/addict wants to become addiction-free would represent one important factor in being admitted. Originally, only those desperate for treatment were accepted. Today, this still seems true for the most part. Merely the length and basic nature of the classic form of therapeutic-community treatment call for high resolve.

Such classic treatment requires living within a tightly disciplined, heavily demanding community for eight to twelve months or more, a community absolutely free of any drugs or alcohol. In recent years, some shorter residential programs of three months or more, and some nonresidential, outpatient programs, have been introduced by organizations specializing in therapeutic-community treatment.

If your alcoholic/addict were not accepted in a therapeutic-community program in the assessment stage, he or she would be referred to sources of treatment that might better meet his or her needs. Reasons for rejection (besides not being desperate enough for treatment) might include having needs due to problems of physical or mental health that the program could not meet, or posing a possible danger to other patients.

[Therapeutic-Community Advantages]

Basic features of a classic therapeutic-community program might offer special advantages for your alcoholic/addict. Overall, such a program would bring very powerful motivating influences to bear on changing his or her fundamental behavior patterns, capabilities, and character. In other words, it could probably change a treacherous, hopeless social outcast into a considerate, responsible, principled, hardworking, self-supporting member of society.

• Assigned Responsibilities

More specifically, your alcoholic/addict would be influenced in such a program to develop sound work habits by long, daily work assignments that help the program facility. These would be graduated from menial to more complex and responsible, fostering self-respect and a strong work ethic. Assignments to run the community's activities and quarters reflect a typically strong self-help emphasis in the program.

• Group Therapy

Group therapy sessions of the "encounter" or confrontational variety can help break down denial of the addiction. They would also help break down deep-seated, negative alcoholic/addict attitudes. Peer support in the program would bolster the abysmal self-esteem of your alcoholic/addict. It would also help him or her accept compassion, and later to bestow it. Family therapy in the program would start mending old dysfunctional relationships.

Education in the program would reveal the truth about addiction's hideous effects on bodies and lives, and would help develop strategies to safeguard abstinence from alcohol and drugs. Counseling for personal guidance would be provided.

Staff counselors and group-therapy leaders would include ex-addicts. Often, they are graduates of the program themselves, men and women with essentially the same addicted experiences as the patients. Other staff members include such professionals as psychologists and social workers specialized in treating chemical dependence.

Teenagers are encouraged to carry on their high school education, while adults would be helped to get appropriate job training. Vocational guidance and job placement services would also be offered.

• Live-In Exposure to Recovery

Moreover, your alcoholic/addict would typically be a live-in member of this tight-knit community for eight to twelve months or more, as noted earlier. That's eight to twelve times longer than the twenty-eight days typical of the full-blown, inpatient, alcholism/addiction rehab treatment programs described in chapter 2. And then, beyond the live-in eight to twelve months, your alcoholic/addict would pursue an aftercare program for some months more.

In sum, "The basic goal of a TC [therapeutic community] is to offer a lifestyle which includes drug abstinence, elimination of anti-social (criminal) behavior, development of employable skills, and the acquisition of positive attitudes, values, and behaviors which reflect honesty, responsibility, non-violence, and self-reliance." That's a statement of the Therapeutic Communities of America, the national membership organization of such agencies providing substance-abuse treatment.[1]

[How to Find a Therapeutic-Community Program]

To locate a possible therapeutic-community program for your alcoholic/addict, you might start with two of the largest and oldest organizations providing them. Daytop Village, one of the two, operates a number of treatment sites in New York, New Jersey, Texas, and California. Phoenix House, another provider, offers programs in New York, Florida, Texas, and California. Both are nonprofit organizations.

Information on the many programs of the Daytop Village organization (usually called simply Daytop) can be obtained from its toll-free telephone hotline, which is 1-800-2-DAYTOP (1-800-232-9867).[2]

Information on Phoenix House programs, as well as on other therapeutic-community programs in your locale, is offered through a hotline phone service affiliated with the Phoenix House Foundation. You can reach this service at the following number (which you can call toll-free from anywhere in the United States, twenty-four hours a day): 1-800-DRUGHELP (1-800-378-4435).[3]

Crisis intervention help and referrals to local sources of crisis services for alcoholics/addicts are also provided by this DRUG-HELP hotline. In addition, you or the alcoholic/addict could get referrals not only to local therapeutic-community programs but to other types of treatment and assistance, too. DRUGHELP also gives information and brief counseling on substance abuse as requested. It keeps all calls strictly confidential.

You could also learn about and communicate with either Daytop or Phoenix House at their Internet sites on the World Wide Web:

http://www.daytop.org
http://www.phoenixhouse.org

As an alternative, you can obtain referrals to therapeutic-community programs in your vicinity through the similar alcoholism/addiction hotline of the U.S. Government, as explained in chapter 2 (1-800-729-6686).

A therapeutic-community program to which you're referred might be operating locally rather than coast-to-coast, as with Daytop or Phoenix House. Hundreds of programs are sponsored locally and adapted to local needs, with more than four hundred programs in the United States and Canada belonging to the Therapeutic Communities of America, their membership organization. They have wide varieties of names—among them, Samaritan, Gateway, Marathon, Village South, and Walden.[4]

Should you happen to locate a therapeutic-community program through a source other than those just discussed, take care that its major purpose is to treat substance abuse. Especially in Britain and elsewhere outside the United States, the term "therapeutic-community" is also applied to residential programs designed to treat mental illnesses rather than alcoholism/addiction.[5]

Also take care, insofar as possible, to pick a therapeutic-community program that is state-licensed and is run by state-licensed professionals. In inquires and visits, be especially alert for signs of destructive harshness going beyond helpful rigor.

There's a fair chance that before you find a therapeutic-community program, your alcoholic/addict would be pressured to enter one by someone with a good deal more authority than you. For example, Phoenix House notes that prospective entrants are referred to it by "probation officers, local court systems, and employers," as well as by schools, doctors, social workers, and psychologists. Some are also referred by friends, while some others learn of Phoenix House by word of mouth.[6]

Your alcoholic/addict might even enter a therapeutic-community program as a prison inmate. Though still relatively rare among all American prisons, such programs have been spreading rapidly throughout the detention system in recent years. In just ten years, for example, from 1987 to 1997, prison-based therapeutic communities in the United States grew from 25 to 110.[7]

• Cost

Government funds and charitable donations might finance treatment for your alcoholic/addict in a therapeutic-community program outside of prison. Some patients in these programs have been so devastated by addiction that they have no money at all. Patients like this are treated without charge.

Financial support for its treatment, Phoenix House says, comes from "a combination of federal, state, and county funds, direct client fees, third-party payments, corporate and foundation grants, and private contributions, and is insurance reimbursable." No charge is made for its initial assessments, but the charge for treatment at one of its residential facilities is $1,500 a month.[8]

Government and charitable funds might finance such treatment for your alcoholic/addict in continuation of such funding from the early days of this type of treatment. Therapeutic-community treatment was originated in a program called Synanon. It was founded in 1958 by a charismatic leader, Charles Dederich, who himself had started recovery in AA and who built extreme adaptations of some elements in AA into the Synanon program.

Daytop's founding in 1963 was inspired by Synanon. Phoenix House was formed in 1968 with Daytop's help and former Synanon residents on its staff. Daytop's name was adopted as an acronym for Drug Addicts Treated on Parole. (The added letter *y* makes it easier to say.) Its primary founder, Joseph Shelly, was the chief probation officer in Brooklyn, New York, and first sought to develop a program to improve results with drug addicts on probation.[9]

Your alcoholic/addict has the American epidemics of heroin addiction in the 1950s and of cocaine and crack-cocaine addiction in the 1960s to thank for these three pioneering therapeutic-community programs. It was in large part to help victims of these alarming epidemics recover that the programs were developed.

Their dramatic success in helping hard-core drug addicts recover—hundreds in Synanon (which no longer functions as a program to help alcoholics/addicts begin recovery),[10] many tens of thousands by now in Daytop and Phoenix House[11]—attracted government and charitable funds for their work. No previous treatment for drug addiction had ever before produced results on such a scale.

[**High Chances for Recovery**]

Your alcoholic/addict has very good chances of both starting and staying in recovery from alcoholism/addiction through a therapeutic-community program—on one condition. That is: completing the program, all the way through to the end. And in a classic therapeutic-community program, this can mean eight months, twelve months, even fifteen months of living in the community, followed by more months in aftercare.

As an example, Daytop reports that "approximately eighty-eight percent of those who complete the program are drug-free and employed up to four years later," according to studies by the National Institute on Drug Abuse and by Daytop itself.[12]

Studies of the various alcoholism/addiction recovery programs—from AA through counseling techniques and alcoholism rehabs to therapeutic communities—generally find that the longer anyone in any type of program achieves abstinence, the better his or her chances are to go on succeeding in recovery. In the end, time can be on the side of your alcoholic/addict—and on your side, too.

[*Epilogue*]

Essentials/Safeguards
for Staying in Recovery

For the alcoholic/addict who concerns you, staying in recovery absolutely counts just as much as getting started in recovery. The better informed you are about what your alcoholic/addict needs for continued recovery, the more powerfully you might reinforce his or her efforts.

[On the Bright Side, Better Lives Than Ever Before]

By now, you might wish that all the effort and strain that it took to get into recovery were over for you and your alcoholic/addict, that you could forget about the whole thing, that your alcoholic/addict's problem would be ended forever, fixed for all time.

However, alcoholism/addiction doesn't work that way. Those who know it best—up close and personal—are the millions of women and men in Alcoholics Anonymous. Medical scientists are still working to define all the biological, psychiatric, and social complexities of the malady. But those in AA know that for all practical purposes—like survival—the disease of alcoholism/addiction has these key features, unless arrested:

- incurable
- progressive
- fatal

Each feature is illustrated by at least one memorable, time-honored AA saying. For incurable: "Once you're a pickle, you can never go back to being a cucumber." For progressive: "The elevator only goes down, never up—but you can get off at any floor." For fatal: "Our disease wants you dead, but it will settle for miserable."

The truths behind sayings like these stem from the direct experience of thousands upon thousands of addicts whom AA members have known personally. Some people they've known never started in recovery at all and died in not too many years. Some started but then relapsed and drank or drugged again and died. Some started and continued in recovery for as long as twenty or thirty years, but then grew complacent and relapsed and died.

Every year a few who relapse make it back into recovery. They report that drinking or drugging again had inflicted as much hellish misery as (or even more than) they'd known when they'd hit bottom before.

On the bright side, though, most AA members some five years or more from their last drink or drug often say they've found a better life in recovery than they ever had before. "Don't drink and go to meetings, and it gets better," new arrivals in AA are assured by those who arrived earlier. Old-timers often add, "It keeps going on, getting better and better. I have a life today beyond anything I ever dreamed of."

You can verify all this for yourself, if you want. Just go to Open AA Meetings. You'll hear speaker after speaker say things exactly like this.

Such a better life can be won by your family member or friend who's an alcoholic/addict starting in recovery. And you can help him or her win it by knowing, and reinforcing, these essentials.

[Don't Drink or Drug, One Day at a Time]

The one overarching requirement for staying in recovery proves virtually impossible for most people to understand. It is this:

The individual who has developed the disease of alcoholism/ addiction must not ingest any alcohol or drugs life-long in order to keep the disease from ruining and finally taking his or her life.

People who drink normally see absolutely no reason why anyone can't stop drinking when it's important to do so. Important reasons not to drink might concern a person's family or job or even physical safety. After all, normal drinkers stop when they need to for just such reasons.

Incredibly, though, alcoholics/addicts do not respond in this way. Controls that stop ruinous drinking or drugging in normal people simply do not function in alcoholics/addicts.

• *Permanent Changes in Brain Chemistry*
What most people don't know—and what is vital for an alcoholic/ addict to know—is that the disease of alcoholism/addiction results in permanent physical changes in the body and brain of the alcoholic/addict. Especially relevant research in recent years has shown

that the brain chemistry of the alcoholic/addict becomes permanently altered.

How that brain chemistry has changed concerns certain neurotransmitter chemicals in the brain. These control such crucial inner emotional states of the individual as ecstatic contentment or agonized discomfort.

At least one enormously important practical effect of these changes is established beyond question: a detoxified alcoholic/addict who has become alcohol-free and drug-free, and who drinks or drugs again, *even a little*, will almost certainly soon see his or her addiction return just as furiously, or more so.

Reverting to alcohol or drug use triggers that altered brain chemistry. That chemistry puts the actively using alcoholic/addict in a state of unbearable distress, a craving relieved (but only to a decreasing extent) by ingesting more and more and more alcohol or drugs.

• *The First Drink*

Recovering alcoholics/addicts remind themselves of their need to use no alcohol or drugs whatever by the saying "It's the first drink that gets you drunk—not the tenth or the twelfth." They also warn each other of "the insanity of the first drink." The experience of many thousands of other alcoholics/addicts they've known shows that it is literally insane for anyone in recovery to imagine that he or she can safely have any alcohol or drugs again.

Recovering women and men have another memorable saying about the danger of the first drink. It was mentioned in chapter 1, but bears repeating here: "When you get hit by a train," they say, "it isn't the caboose that kills you. It's the locomotive."

• *One Day at a Time*

A practice especially helpful at the start of recovery has long been widespread in Alcoholics Anonymous. It can feel intolerable for newly sober alcoholics/addicts to think they can never have any alcohol or drugs for the rest of their lives. Instead, as seasoned AA members suggest to the newcomer, just resolve not to drink or drug today. Don't drink or drug today, they suggest, and get to an AA meeting tonight.

They may add about themselves, "I don't know whether or not I'll drink tomorrow. What I do know is that I won't drink today. Each day I decide I just won't drink today. We stay sober just one day at a time."

And newcomers in AA find in many cases that they are able to refrain from drink or drugs just for today, no matter what happens. To do so, they also use the many other kinds of help offered in AA. How many newcomers succeed in applying the one-day-at-a-time method? There are no conclusive studies on this question. But an approximate answer is—thousands, many thousands, of men and women worldwide who start out in AA every day.

• *Medications*

Anyone starting in recovery from alcoholism/addiction needs to exercise great care concerning drugs used for medical purposes. Some substantial numbers of persons starting recovery have been addicted to medical drugs. Very often, these persons include physicians, nurses, and other health-care professionals. Many others are very anxious women and men who had become addicted to "minor tranquilizers" like Valium.

Among types of medical drugs used by such addicts are:

- **tranquilizers,** like Valium, for anxiety and tension (as just noted);
- **sedatives** for sleeplessness, like Seconal and other barbiturates;
- **stimulants,** like Dexedrine or Ritalin (sometimes prescribed for weight loss); and
- **narcotics,** powerful prescription painkillers, like Demerol, Dilaudid, or Percocet.

Persons who had been addicted to any such drugs need to make every effort to stay away from these when in recovery. And anyone in recovery should never take any of them without observing the precautions that follow. An experienced counselor or therapist specializing in substance abuse can best advise an alcoholic/addict on these precautions. So can long-experienced and broadly informed recovering alcoholics/addicts in AA or similar organizations. In summary, the major precautions to act on if you are an alcoholic/addict in recovery are:

1. Tell each physician, dentist, or other individual providing any of your health care that you are an alcoholic/addict in recovery, and that you absolutely want to avoid taking any habit-forming medicines to the greatest extent possible. Be especially sure to do this as soon as any anesthesia is proposed for you. However, minor local anesthetics given by injection, such as novocain for dental work, pose no risk.

2. Never use any mouthwashes or nonprescription medicines containing any alcohol. Remedies for coughs and colds especially often have high alcohol content. Scrutinize labels listing ingredients before using.

3. Tell the one or two persons closest to you—and especially your sponsor in AA (or similar support group)—of any possibly addictive medicines recommended for you, before you take them.

4. If narcotic or other highly addictive drugs are medically necessary in the judgment of your doctor, tell your sponsor or the person closest to you (and preferably have that individual hold the drug and dispense each dosage to you), take the drug only exactly as prescribed, take the drug only so long as your doctor tells you it's necessary, and throw away any supply of the drug remaining as soon as you stop taking it.

• Medicines to Treat Mental Illness Are Not Only Safe, but Can Be Essential

One broad type of medicines used to alter states of mind and emotion is quite safe for you if you're a recovering alcoholic/addict. They can even prove essential to recovery in some cases. These are almost all of the kinds of drugs used to treat mental illnesses.

As many as half of all persons with serious mental illnesses also become alcoholics/addicts, authoritative studies have found. As a result, some people who start recovery from alcoholism/addiction also suffer from mental illnesses.

Those mental illnesses seem most commonly to be clinical depression or bipolar disorder (which used to have the more descriptive name of "manic depression"). Also among them are anxiety disorders that include phobias, panic attacks, obsessive-compulsive disorder, and post-traumatic stress disorder.

Drugs that need to be taken regularly over the years to keep such mental illnesses in check pose no danger to recovery when their use is prescribed and monitored by a psychiatrist knowledgeable about alcoholism/addiction. In fact, use of such drugs may be needed by some persons in order to keep the distress of the mental illness at bay enough to enable that person to stay in recovery.

Avoid Tranquilizers and Sedatives: However, recovering alcoholics/ addicts needing treatment for an additional mental illness should be wary of two kinds of drugs prescribed at times by some psychiatrists and other physicians. These are tranquilizers for anxiety, and sedatives for sleeplessness.

Before agreeing to take either kind of these drugs, the individual should try all other possible means of relieving the condition. And if either seems absolutely necessary, it should be taken only temporarily and precisely as prescribed—and then stopped as soon as possible. Moreover, counseling and alternative medications that do not pose risks and often bring relief can be located by consulting chemical dependency specialists.

In many cases, severe depression and anxiety develop as part of the disease of alcoholism/addiction. Accordingly, an alcoholic/addict starting recovery may find in time that such depression and anxiety do not need any psychiatric treatment because they are gradually relieved by recovery itself.

Stop the Addiction First: Alcoholism/addiction can either mimic or mask the symptoms of mental illness in some persons. For addicts thus afflicted, stopping all alcohol and drugs often proves necessary before an accurate diagnosis concerning mental illness can be made.

Persons in recovery hear time and again how some of their fellow alcoholics/addicts thought they had suffered from a mental illness like depression or panic disorder, and spent years in psychotherapy for relief. They continued in their addiction, though, often never even telling their therapists the facts of their alcohol or drug abuse. Their years in therapy also failed to improve their condition.

Successful Treatment: Others among them found that their symptoms (like severe depression or wild mood-swings) continued even after they had stopped using any alcohol or drugs for a few months. These individuals found that, once their addiction had been cleared up in recovery, they could accept and follow psychiatric treatment for the mental illness afflicting them in addition to their alcoholism/addiction.

Before, their raging alcoholism/addiction had made them unable to start or continue in psychiatric treatment. Their addiction needed to be stopped first in recovery before psychiatric treatment could make any progress with them.

Psychiatrists and psychotherapists well-informed about alcoholism/addiction today often recognize patients like this. Once these professionals diagnose the alcoholism/addiction in addition to the mental illness, they tell such a patient that they can be of no help until after the patient starts recovery from the alcoholism/addiction.

[Stay Vigilant at All Times]

A second vital requirement for remaining in recovery is for alcoholics/addicts to stay vigilant at all times against any possible dangers of taking a drink or a drug. Their need for such constant vigilance stems from the permanently changed brain chemistry caused by their alcoholism/addiction.

In the days, weeks, and even months of early recovery, this altered brain chemistry may inflict an intense craving for alcohol and/

or drugs. But in time such persistent cravings lessen or vanish entirely for most who continue in recovery.

However, those changes in brain chemistry result in permanent vulnerability to seemingly automatic impulses to take a drink or a drug. Such impulses can come especially often in early sobriety. But they also never completely go away. Even after as many as twenty or more years in recovery, in just about every case, the alcoholic/addict will still at times have urges to take a drink or a drug.

Still more alarming is the fact that an unconscious reflex can make one take a drink or a drug at any vulnerable time. This can happen regardless of the number of years in recovery. Greatest risk of such a reflex seems to arise when the alcoholic/addict is either around others who are happily drinking or drugging, or alone, and in absolute surprise comes upon a once-irresistible liquor or drug that can be taken right now in secret.

In such situations, only extreme vigilance can protect recovery. Phoning or meeting with a friend (or sponsor) in recovery is also strongly suggested whenever a reflex, impulse, urge, or craving strikes.

• How to Stay Vigilant in Early Recovery

Alcoholics/addicts maintain their vigilance in early recovery especially by joining with others in recovery and meeting with them preferably every day or at least once a week. Joining with others can be done in an aftercare program following detox and rehab, or in an ongoing therapy group treating substance abuse, or in AA or a similar recovery organization. Often, an individual finds it helpful to combine aftercare or ongoing therapy with AA membership.

Joining others seems to work best when the alcoholic/addict accepts the guidance on staying sober of either the therapist or of long-experienced fellow members of AA or a similar program. Newcomers are less able to see how their addicted systems might be leading them unconsciously to drink or drug again than experienced members, who can recognize, warn of, and help defend against such dangers.

• Keep Alcohol and Drugs Out of the Home

Vigilance is also promoted by changing habits and actions that had been associated with one's active drinking and/or drugging. One of the first changes suggested is to get rid of any liquor or drugs in one's home immediately, and to keep them out. Doing this can protect against a passing but instantly acute impulse to get high. It also helps remind one of the need for vigilance.

It is also suggested to newcomers in recovery that it's wise for them to stay away as much as possible from people, places, and things that had been associated with their alcoholism/addiction. Being around the companions, places, and articles that had been connected with getting high might bring on cravings that completely overwhelm one's vigilance.

Professionals treating alcoholics/addicts similarly suggest making a list of situations that could bring on cravings or impulses—for instance, needing to relax after a very hard day. Professionals then suggest adding to each situation listed a planned response that would deflate any craving or even avoid the situation.

Avoiding stress is also suggested as an aid to staying vigilant. In AA, for example, use of the acronym HALT is urged for avoiding danger. That acronym stands for *Hungry, Angry, Lonely,* or *Tired.* When troubled by any of these states, recognize the risk and correct the cause of that source of stress right away.

• *Staying Vigilant Through Years of Recovery*

Complacence poses the primary threat to recovery after years without alcohol or drugs. Continuing to stay connected to others in recovery and the principles they follow is found by many to be needed for sufficient vigilance against complacency.

Ongoing connection with such others as AA members and groups counters complacency in part by "keeping it green." Hearing from other new members the horror of their last days of raging addiction reminds the person with some years of sobriety of his or her own addicted agonies. That memory may otherwise grow dim or vanish altogether. Denial of how bad it had finally gotten is buried deep in the permanent brain chemistry of even the long-recovering alcoholic/addict.

Remaining connected to friends in recovery and meetings with them also regularly reinforce all the actions and attitudes effective for keeping the disease of alcoholism/addiction in check.

Vigilance may be preserved best of all by helping others to start and stay in recovery. Doing so obviously both keeps the memory very green and reinforces all the necessary principles of recovery.

Continuing to help others get and stay sober seems to have the highest protective power for still other reasons that are not yet well understood. AA calls such efforts "twelfth-step work" of "carrying the message to other alcoholics," as noted in chapter 1. Helping others in this way serves as the bedrock of the AA program for recovery. AA itself began when a fatally diseased alcoholic securities analyst, Bill W., found that he could stay sober only by helping a fatally diseased alcoholic/addict M.D., Dr. Bob S., get and stay sober. AA's founding date is June 10, 1935, the date of Dr. Bob's last drink.

[Start Again, Reinforced, After a Possible Relapse]

Of greatest benefit to a recovering alcoholic/addict is not to have a relapse. In a relapse (or *slip*, as long called in AA), he or she drinks or drugs again, just once or for a while. But some numbers of those in recovery do relapse, as noted earlier. Relapse can happen especially at critical times in early recovery, due to factors like high stress or a return to the grandiose thinking of one's drinking or drugging days.

Someone who does relapse knows both the horrors of addiction and the relief of recovery, and he or she will almost certainly want to resume recovery at some point after the relapse starts.

When that happens, the person should absolutely not let shame or embarrassment or hopelessness block resuming recovery. Instead, he or she absolutely should go back by reentering either treatment or AA or both. Others who have relapsed and returned will help these members especially. All will give the person a warm welcome.

Once back in recovery, he or she might try to feel grateful for having again escaped the agonies and doom of addiction. It's helpful, too, if the person can reinforce his or her recovery by seeing ways in which other actions in recovery could have prevented the relapse. Not to mention how they could prevent relapsing in the future.

• *Living in a Recovery Group Home Could Help Ward Off a Relapse*

If the alcoholic/addict worrying you feels very shaky about abstinence (either in resuming right after a slip, or in early recovery), extra help can be found. Special protection against the possibility of a relapse is provided by a variety of group homes or other residential communities across the country. These are residences specifically for persons in recovery from alcoholism/addiction.

Treatment agencies sponsor a number of such residences. Some operate as halfway houses for alcoholics/addicts who have just completed the agencies' inpatient rehab programs. Others often have the help of local government or charitable support. Recovery residences of this latter kind are usually introduced to serve recovering alcoholics/addicts whose regular homes or neighborhoods are riddled with alcoholism/addiction.

• *High Watch Farm*

Your alcoholic/addict might find a certain group residence for recovery especially appealing for its complete commitment to AA. This is High Watch Farm in the rural town of Kent in western Connecticut.

High Watch was established in 1940 by AA's cofounder, Bill W., and a few of his fellow early members of AA. AA on principle could not (and cannot) own property. High Watch was consequently organized as an independent, nonprofit entity that today describes itself as "the oldest residential treatment community based on the life-changing principles of Alcoholics Anonymous" (according to its home page on the World Wide Web).

Your alcoholic/addict would find that virtually all staff members at High Watch are AA members, and that its program consists of AA meetings, talks on spirituality in AA, informal conversations with others in AA, and quiet reflection amid its two hundred acres of forest and fields. None of its program is conducted by professional therapists, social workers, or counselors.

High Watch "guests" seeking reinforcement of their recovery come mainly from the northeast United States but also from many far-distant locations. Such guests must be over age seventeen. They must stay at least two weeks, but may remain as long as they want. Guests going for just "rest and renewal" must stay at least two nights, and often do so on a weekend. Open AA Meetings at High Watch can be attended by anyone traveling there.

You or your alcoholic/addict can get in touch with High Watch as follows:

High Watch Farm
P.O. Box 607
Kent, CT 06757
Phone: (toll-free) 1-888-HWF-KENT (493-5368),
or 860-927-3772
Web site: http://www.highwatchfarm.com

• *Oxford Houses*

It's far more likely that a different residence offering would be workable for your alcoholic/addict in recovery. Oxford House offers more than six hundred self-supporting recovery group homes that are under the sponsorship of this special private organization.

These Oxford House group homes have been introduced in more than 250 communities in forty-one states, and have over five thousand residents. They have grown from a single Oxford House that opened in Silver Spring, Maryland, in 1975.

"Each House represents a remarkably effective and low-cost method of preventing relapse," says the Oxford House home page. Rent paid by the residents supports each House, and each House is run democratically by its residents, with no resident counselor.

Any one Oxford House has from six to fifteen or more residents, and must be either only for men, only for women, or only for women with children. More than one hundred of the houses are for women. Residents average a stay of slightly over one year, but some continue for four years or more.

Residents can stay indefinitely so long as they remain in good standing by paying their share of costs and using no alcohol or drugs. Drinking or drugging brings immediate expulsion. Less than 20 percent of the residents have had relapses.

Loans of up to four thousand dollars provided under the Federal Anti-Drug Abuse Act of 1988 are available to pay the first month's rent and security deposit for a new Oxford House being organized by a group of future residents. Help in organizing new houses is also provided by Oxford House, Inc., a nonprofit, charitable corporation. Oxford Houses maintain close but unofficial ties with groups and members of AA and Narcotics Anonymous.

Information about individual Oxford Houses and the entire Oxford House system is available as follows:

Oxford House, Inc.
ICA Group Foundation
P.O. Box 994
Great Falls, VA 22066-0994
Phone: Toll-Free 1-800-486-6488 or 703-450-6501
Fax: Toll-Free 1-800-899-6577 or 703-450-6577
TTY (TDD) Service for the Deaf: 703-450-6503
Web site: http://www.icagroup.org/main.html

[Full Knowledge and Encouragement]

Are you the lover, the wife, or the husband of an alcoholic/addict who has started recovery? Or the mom or dad? The son? Daughter?

If so, you may at first feel bitter disappointment rather than relief. This develops quite often, for lovers and spouses especially. It may seem to you that all your devotion and efforts over the years failed to help your loved one. Instead, strangers such as counselors in a treatment program and/or friends in AA accomplished what you could not.

Try to restrain such feelings if they happen to beset you. For one thing, they are essentially part of the old, unknowing ways in which the other's disease of addiction had deeply affected you. You just didn't know that the disease had totally controlled your alcoholic/addict.

For another thing, all your loyalty and love may indeed have been vital in helping influence him or her finally to start recovery. Some of the most moving histories told by those in recovery recount how much something that a beloved little son or daughter had said or done moved them to get help.

Moreover, the actions outlined in this book that you can take to help get him or her started in recovery may be crucial to that recovery. No one really knows what causes an alcoholic/addict to start recovery. But much is known about actions that influence an alcoholic/addict to start. Your actions toward that end are at least better than doing nothing about it. And at best, they may be pivotal.

What actions you take after your alcoholic/addict starts recovery can go far in safeguarding that recovery. Mainly knowing about the disease of alcoholism/addiction, and what's needed to go on recovering from it—and then acting and talking based on that knowledge—represent the most important way you can help.

For an alcoholic/addict, forging ahead in recovery is hard. For you to understand how and why, and to give encouragement and help, might spell the difference between failure and success.

[Ten Key Things You Can Do]

In sum, this book is designed to give you important information about methods and resources known to be effective for moving an alcoholic/addict toward recovery. However, as you may have already discovered, trying to change a severely addicted person can be stressful. At times, it can elicit other debilitating feelings as well—ones like fear, fatigue, depression, and anxiety.

Feeling these negative emotions, though completely normal, can often be an obstacle to helping your alcoholic/addict find recovery, because negative emotions will distort both your perceptions and your thinking. The following list should help you offset the distorting effects of such emotions. It also sums up major points made in the book.

1. **Start with Yourself.** It's likely that you can play an important part in helping your alcoholic/addict start in recovery. However, to do so, you need to be in a healthy condition yourself. You probably won't be able to help if you're not

   To check on your own condition, first look at what's happening to you and focus on your needs. Shift your focus away from the needs of your alcoholic/addict.

   Keep in mind that his or her addictive behavior can greatly affect you. As explained in chapter 3, stop reacting automatically and start tending to your needs. You can control yourself but you can't control the behavior of your alcoholic/addict.

   However, the changes you make in your own behavior can have a powerful influence on the addict's behavior. You should find it helpful to learn from others (like the people you meet in Al-Anon) the true nature of alcoholism/addiction, and how to accept being powerless over it. Once you do this, you will start serving as a role model for your alcoholic/addict as you break through your own denial and progress in your own recovery.

2. **Stop Enabling.** Let the social, legal, and vocational consequences of addicted behavior occur as they will without interfering. (Of course, for life-threatening emergencies, you should immediately seek emergency police or medical help.)

But letting non-life-threatening consequences result unimpeded is an important way for the alcoholic/addict to experience the destructive outcomes of drinking or drugging. This can in turn help motivate your alcoholic/addict to consider changing. You may find it hard at first to stop enabling. But the more you do it, the easier it becomes and the more it helps in the end.

3. **Learn to Detach.** You need to detach from your alcoholic/addict in order to stop enabling. By detaching, you recognize that the problem is caused by your alcoholic/addict alone. You recognize, too, that the problem is one to be solved by your alcoholic/addict, and not by you.

Detaching doesn't mean that you have to stop caring for or about your alcoholic/addict. (In the Al-Anon phrase, you'll recall, one should "detach with love.") Instead, it means that you must distance yourself enough, both emotionally and physically, to allow your alcoholic/addict to experience the consequences of his or her addiction without being rescued by you.

Detaching also calls for you to get help for yourself with

all that you're going through. Without detaching, the needs of your alcoholic/addict become all-consuming while your needs go neglected.

4. **Be Prepared for Emergencies.** Have phone numbers on hand for immediate help with possible medical or police emergencies. (These usually become more likely as alcoholism/addiction progresses.) Such phone numbers and sources of help are given in chapters 1 and 2, and "Sources of Help and Information."

5. **Get Effective Support.** As noted earlier, stress and negative emotions you experience result in distorted perception and thinking. One way to lessen their effects is to develop and use an effective social support system, as in Al-Anon or a family therapy group. Others who have dealt successfully with situations like yours can give you hope, can clarify your perceptions, and can counteract your faulty thinking. Getting effective support can help calm you and pacify your relationship with your alcoholic/addict. This should in time help move your alcoholic/addict toward recovery.

6. **Seek Professional Help.** Arrange professional treatment first for yourself and perhaps for other family members, then for your alcoholic/addict. Seeking help yourself can often open the door for your alcoholic/addict to follow your lead.

Another reason to seek professional help is to gain access to full medical and psychiatric diagnoses. You might recall from chapter 2 that substantial numbers of alcoholics/addicts suffer also from other mental and physical illnesses. Working with a professional can bring you and your alcoholic/addict powerful techniques for recovery from all pathological conditions.

7. **Plan an Intervention.** A carefully planned and executed intervention can be a life-saving endeavor, as explained in chapter 2.

8. **View a Possible Relapse as Part of the Recovery Process.** Family members, lovers, and even some professionals may interpret a relapse of your alcoholic/addict as a failure of recovery. However, in many cases, an alcoholic/addict who has relapsed eventually achieves a sustained recovery. Such alcoholics/addicts often see their relapses as experiences that helped clarify their need for more serious commitment to recovery. Should your alcoholic/addict have a relapse, it could be most important for you to urge her or him to set all guilt or shame aside and get back into recovery as soon as possible.

9. **Spirituality May Really Help.** As discussed in chapter 3 especially, keep an open mind toward using spirituality as conceived in Al-Anon and AA to counter alcoholism/addiction. In those fellowships, you and your alcoholic/addict could learn how such spirituality often proves an essential help to others in their recoveries. An understanding of such spirituality and its power usually comes slowly, and with practice, in those fellowships.

10. **Don't Give Up.** Your alcoholic/addict may need more than one course of treatment or entry into AA (or NA or CA) in order to win through to a stable recovery. But you can make a crucial difference in his or her chances by staying involved and active. Research and experience alike show that alcoholics/addicts enter recovery when they're ready. But you can mightily help your alcoholic/addict become ready—not by bailing him or her out of trouble, but by believing in the individual and consistently showing the way to recovery.

Notes

**Introduction: The Problem: Enormous; Heart-Breaking—
But You Can Have Great Rewards Ahead**

1. Mateo Falco, *The Making of a Drug-Free America* (New York: Times Books/Random House, 1992), 180–181.
2. Ibid., 3.

Prologue: Sure Signs of the Disease of Alcoholism/Addiction

1. David Maraniss, *First in His Class: A Biography of Bill Clinton* (New York: Simon & Schuster, 1995), 405–423.
2. Dennis Wholey, *The Courage to Change* (New York: Warner Books, 1984), 153–169.
3. Betty Ford, with Chris Chase, *Betty: A Glad Awakening* (Garden City: Doubleday, 1987).
4. George McGovern, *Terry: My Daughter's Life-and-Death Struggle with Alcoholism* (New York: Villard Books, 1996).
5. Reprinted with permission of A.A. World Services, from the pamphlet "Is A.A. for you? Twelve questions only you can answer." (New York: 1973). © 1973 by A.A. World Services, Inc. See also p. iv.
6. Allen Frances, M.D., and Michael B. First, M.D., *Your Mental Health: A Layman's Guide to the Psychiatrist's Bible* (New York: Scribner, 1999), 121–122. Reprinted with the permission of Scribner, a Division of Simon & Schuster. © 1999 by Dr. Allen Frances and Dr. Michael B. First. In their book, readers are cautioned as follows: "Consult your physician before acting on any information in this book."

Notes

Chapter One—The AA Way: Carrying the Message
(After Having Invented It)

1. AA General Service Office, "Membership," http://www.alcoholics-anonymous.org [cited 17 May 2000].
2. Ibid.
3. Frances and First, *Your Mental Health*, 147.
4. George E. Vaillant, *The Natural History of Alcoholism Revisited* (Cambridge, Mass.: Harvard University Press, 1995), 388. Reprinted with permission of the publisher. See also p. iv.
5. Anonymous, *Alcoholics Anonymous, Third Edition* (New York: Alcoholics Anonymous World Services, 1976), 18. Reprinted with the permission of Alcoholics Anonymous World Services. © 1939, 1955, 1976 by Alcoholics Anonymous World Services. See also p. iv.

Chapter Two—The Professional Way:
Intervention, Detox, Rehab, Aftercare

1. Two major originators, of this method, William R. Miller and Stephen Rollnick, discuss it at length in their book, *Motivational Interviewing* (New York: Guilford Press, 1991).
2. Marc Galanter, "Network Therapy," in *Psychotherapy and Substance Abuse: A Practitioner's Handbook* by Arnold M. Washton (New York: Guilford Press, 1995), 357–371.
3. Project MATCH Research Group, "Matching Patients with Alcohol Disorders to Treatments: Clinical Implications from Project MATCH," *Journal of Mental Health* 7, no. 6 (1998): 589–602.
4. Department of Health and Human Services, Substance Abuse and Mental Health Administration, *Making Your Workplace Drug Free: A Kit for Employers, Employer Tip Sheet #10* (Rockville, Md.: no date).

Chapter Three—The Al-Anon Way: To Stop Enabling; To Detach with Love

1. Al-Anon Family Group Headquarters, *This Is Al-Anon*, pamphlet P-32 (Virginia Beach, Va.: Al-Anon Family Group Headquarters, Inc., 1998), 3.
2. Al-Anon Family Group Headquarters, *The Twelve Steps and Traditions*, pamphlet P-17 (Virginia Beach, Va.: Al-Anon Family Group Headquarters, Inc., 1986), 10.
3. *Anonymous, Alcoholics Anonymous, Third Edition* (New York: Alcoholics Anonymous World Services, Inc., 1976) Anonymous, 59–60.
4. Al-Anon Family Group Headquarters, *The Al-Anon Family Groups, Classic Edition* (Virginia Beach, Va.: Al-Anon Family Group Headquarters, 2000). Reprinted with the permission of Al-Anon Family Group Headquarters. © 2000 by Al-Anon Family Group Headquarters. See also p. iv.
5. *How Al-Anon Works for Families and Friends of Alcoholics* (Virginia Beach, Va.: Al-Anon Family Group Headquarters, Inc., 1995), 84.
6. Ibid., 85–86.
7. *This Is Al-Anon*, pamphlet P-32 (Virginia Beach, Va.: Al-Anon Family Group Headquarters, Inc., 1998), 3.
8. Ibid., 3–4.

Chapter Four—The Work-Life Way: Programs to Start Recovery for Employees or Professionals

1. Alcohol and Drug Abuse and Mental Health Administration, *Economic Costs of Alcohol and Drug Abuse and Mental Illness* (Rockville, Md.: Department of Health and Human Services, 1990).
2. Jeffrey Weisberg and Gene Hawes, *Rx for Recovery* (New York: Franklin Watts, 1989), 250–251.
3. Commission on Lawyer Assistance Programs (CoLAP), of the American Bar Association, "History of CoLAP," http://www.abanet.org/cpr/colap/home.html [cited 15 April 2000].

4. Larry Smith, "Passing the Bar . . . Celebrating the Tenth Anniversary of an ABA Triumph," *Of Counsel* 21, September 1998.
5. Ibid.
6. Robert Holman Coombs, *Drug-Impaired Professionals* (Cambridge, Mass.: Harvard University Press, 1997), 272.

Chapter Five—The Law-Enforcement Way: Drunk-Driving Arrests, Drug Courts, Prison Programs

1. Mim J. Landry, *Overview of Addiction Treatment Effectiveness* (Rockville, Md.: Department of Health and Human Services, 1997), 83.
2. Laura M. Maruschak, *DWI Offenders Under Correctional Supervision*, Department of Justice, Bureau of Justice Statistics, June 1999.
3. Department of Justice, Drug Court Clearinghouse and Technical Assistance Project, *Looking at a Decade of Drug Courts* (Washington, D.C.: GPO, 1998).
4. Department of Justice, Office of Justice Programs, *Attorney General Reno Announces Funds to Continue Successful Drug Court Program*, press release, 3 June 1999.
5. Christopher S. Wren, "Arizona Finds Cost Savings in Treating Drug Offenders," *New York Times*, 21 April 1999, p. A14.
6. Evelyn Nieves, "California Gets Set to Shift on Sentencing Drug Users," *New York Times*, 10 November 2000, http://www.nytimes.com/2000/11/10/politics.
7. Katherine E. Finkelstein, "New York to Offer Most Addicts Treatment Instead of Jail Terms," *New York Times*, 23 June 2000, http://www.nytimes.com/library/national/regional.
8. Richard Perez-Pena, "Pataki Presents Plan to Ease Laws on Drugs," *New York Times*, 17 January 2001, http://www.nytimes.com/2001/01/17/nyregion. James C. McKinley, Jr., "Signs of a Drug War Thaw," *New York Times*, 21 January 2001, p. 29.
9. Timothy Egan, "Less Crime, More Criminals," *New York Times*, 7 March 1999, sec. 4, p. 1.
10. Fox Butterfield, "Drug Treatment Drops as Use Rises, Study Finds," *New York Times*, 6 January 1999, p. A14.

Notes

11. Robert Mathias, "Correctional Treatment Helps Offenders Stay Drug and Arrest Free," *NIDA Notes* (July/August 1995).
12. "Inmates Take Initiative of Fixing School Computers," *Delaware Voice*, http://www.delawareonline.com [cited 26 March 2000].
13. Douglas S. Lipton, *The Effectiveness of Treatment for Drug Abusers under Criminal Justice Supervision*. Washington, D.C.: U.S. Department of Justice, 1995.
14. Douglas S. Lipton. "Drug Abuse Treatment in the Criminal Justice System: Is Drug Treatment in Jeopardy?" *Connection* (June 1996).

Chapter Six—The Therapeutic-Community Way: Daytop, Phoenix House, Samaritan, Others

1. Therapeutic Communities of America, "About TCA," http://www.tcanet.org/about.htm [cited 13 April 2000].
2. Daytop Village, "Daytop for a Drug-Free World," http://www.daytop.org [cited 13 April 2000].
3. American Council for Drug Education, "drughelp.org, About Our Services," http://www.drughelp.org/service/service/htm [cited 6 May 2000].
4. Therapeutic Communities of America, "About TCA."
5. David Kennard, *An Introduction to Therapeutic Communities* (London: Jessica Kingsley Publishers, 1998).
6. Phoenix House, "Phoenix House: An Overview," http://www.phoenixhouse.org/programs/about/index.htm [cited 13 April 2000].
7. Kennard, *An Introduction to Therapeutic Communities*, 83.
8. "Phoenix House."
9. Monsignor William B. O'Brien and Ellis Henican, *You Can't Do It Alone: The Daytop Way to Make Your Child Drug-Free* (New York: Simon & Schuster, 1993), 44–52.
10. O'Brien and Henican, *You Can't Do It Alone*, 63.
11. "Daytop" and "Phoenix House."
12. "Daytop."

Sources of Help and Information via Internet, Phone, Fax, Mail, and Print

This section is designed to serve as your quick reference for getting help for an alcoholic/addict who concerns you—and for getting help for yourself. For your convenience, it includes the sources of help given in the text of the book as well as additional sources of help and information.

Chapter One. The AA Way: Carrying the Message
(After Having Invented It)

• To Find Nearby AA Groups or the Central Office
You need only look in your local phone directory to reach AA throughout the United States. You'll find "AA" or "Alcoholics Anonymous" listed in the directory's white pages under businesses and organizations (rather than residences). An AA phone number may be listed in the directory's yellow pages (classified phone directory listings), under a heading like "Alcoholism Information and Treatment Centers."

Local police also often could tell you where and when nearby AA meetings are held.

If you're outside the United States, you can similarly try local phone directories. You can also use the following telephone numbers, mailing address, and World Wide Web home page address. (In the United States, you can also use these additional phone numbers and addresses.)

Alcoholics Anonymous World Services, Inc. (the AA General Service Office for the United States and Canada, as well as the publisher of official AA literature and coordinator of AA worldwide):

Sources of Help and Information

Mailing address: P.O. Box 459, New York, NY 10163

Phone: 212-870-3400

Web site: http://www.aa.org

(This site also has links to AA "intergroup" telephone information services for many metropolitan areas and regions of the United States and Canada. It also gives information for contacting International General Service Offices of AA around the world.)

Internet "on-line" AA meetings, and other Internet sites on AA: You or your alcoholic/addict can also join in AA meetings that are conducted on-line on the Internet. Some are held by exchange of e-mail messages; others, called "real-time" on-line meetings, follow a chat-room format. You can access the source for these on-line AA meetings as follows: http://www.aa-intergroup.org.

A great many other Internet sites on the World Wide Web concerning AA are available. You can locate these with any Web search engine software available to you, by searching on "Alcoholics Anonymous" and "AA."

* **To Find Local Groups and Central Offices of Narcotics Anonymous (NA) and Cocaine Anonymous (CA)**

You can find groups of NA or CA in your locale in the local telephone directories in some areas, or by contacting their central offices below.

Narcotics Anonymous World Service

Mailing address: P.O. Box 9999, Van Nuys, CA 91409

Phone: 818-773-9999

Fax: 818-700-0700

Web site: http://www.na.org

Sources of Help and Information

Cocaine Anonymous World Services Office

Mailing address: CAWSO, Inc., P.O. Box 2000, Los Angeles,
CA 90049-8000
Phone: 310-559-5833
Fax: 310-559-2554
Web site: http://www.ca.org

• To Find Special Groups of Professionals in Recovery

Professionals in a number of fields who are in AA and/or otherwise in
recovery have formed special groups. Representatives of a number of these
groups have formed the "Council of Special Mutual Help Groups." The
council maintains a World Wide Web site with brief information about
itself and with hypertext links giving access to the Web home pages of
each member group. Member groups are for professions that include nursing, anesthesiology, pharmacy, medicine, clergy, academics, psychologists,
social workers, and veterinarians.

Web site: http://www.crml.uab.edu/~jah

• Official AA Publications

AA's World Services Office publishes and distributes a number of books,
a large number of pamphlets, and a monthly magazine, *The Grapevine.*
All are available from the General Service Office and at least some should
be available at almost any Open AA Meeting you might attend. The books
and pamphlets are official AA publications, "conference-approved" (that
is, approved by a conference of delegates in AA's structure of representatives from the individual AA groups to the national and international
levels). Major AA books include:

*Alcoholics Anonymous: The Story of How Many Thousands of Men and
Women Have Recovered from Alcoholism.* Third Edition. (New York: Alcoholics Anonymous World Services, Inc., 1976). The original and still
central AA work, setting forth the AA program. Traditionally called "the
big book" in AA.

Dr. Bob and the Good Old-Timers: A Biography and Recollections of Early

A.A. in the Midwest (New York: Alcoholics Anonymous World Services, Inc., 1980). An official biography of Dr. Bob S., co-founder of AA, and an account of the early origins of AA.

"Pass It On": The Story of Bill Wilson and How the A.A. Message Reached the World (New York: Alcoholics Anonymous World Services, Inc., 1984). An official biography of Bill W., co-founder of AA, and an account of the origins and growth of AA.

Twelve Steps and Twelve Traditions (New York: Alcoholics Anonymous World Services, Inc., 1952). Explains in detail the twelve steps of the AA program for individual members, and the twelve traditions or basic principles for the guidance of AA groups and the AA organization overall.

• Other Books About AA or About Alcoholism/Addiction and Recovery

Among a great many books about alcoholism/addiction and recovery from it, or about AA, the following may be of special interest to readers of this book.

Kathleen Whalen Fitzgerald, *Alcoholism: The Genetic Inheritance* (New York: Doubleday, 1988). An especially clear explanation for lay readers of alcoholism as a disease.

Frances Hartigan, *Bill W.: A Biography of Alcoholics Amonymous Co-founder Bill Wilson* (New York: St. Martin's/Thomas Dunne Books, 2000). A recent independent biography.

James R. Milam, Ph.D., and Katherine Ketcham, *Under the Influence: A Guide to the Myths and Realities of Alcoholism* (New York: Bantam, 1983). A widely admired book for lay readers on the nature of alcoholism and effective treatment for it.

Nan Robertson, *Getting Better: Inside Alcoholics Anonymous* (New York: William Morrow & Co., 1988). An independent but sympathetic and searching account of AA by a Pulitzer Prize–winning journalist.

George E. Vaillant, *The Natural History of Alcoholism* (1983), and *The Natural History of Alcoholism Revisited* (1995), Cambridge, Mass.: Harvard University Press. Two highly readable reports on an unparalleled, rigorously scientific, forty-year study of alcoholism in a large group of men in the northeastern United States.

Jeffrey Weisberg, M.D., and Gene Hawes, *Rx for Recovery: The Medical and Health Guide for Alcoholics, Addicts, and Their Families* (New York: Franklin Watts, 1989). Explains for lay readers the physical bases of alcoholism/addiction and its harm to the body, and advises on medical and health aspects of getting and staying sober and drug-free.

• **Books Relating Personal Life-Stories of Alcoholism/Addiction and Recovery**
Firsthand reports on alcoholism/addiction and recovery are available in a great many books. AA's "big book," *Alcoholics Anonymous*, introduced such accounts and carries forty-two of them, written by wide varieties of persons, in its third edition. Many books with similar reports can be found by searching under *alcoholism* or *addiction* in library catalogs. A very few such books of special or current interest are as follows.

Betty Ford and Chris Chase, *Betty: A Glad Awakening* (Garden City, N.Y.: Doubleday, 1987). The wife of U.S. President Gerald Ford tells how she became an alcoholic/addict in the White House, went through an intervention by her family, entered recovery, and founded a major alcoholism/addiction treatment center in California.

Caroline Knapp, *Drinking: A Love Story* (New York: Bantam Doubleday Dell, 1996). A woman journalist vividly portrays her alcoholism/addiction and recovery through an affluent upbringing and career.

Dennis Wholley, *The Courage to Change: Hope and Help for Alcoholics and Their Families* (Boston: Houghton Mifflin, 1984). Remarkable for its accounts by many celebrities of the day who are alcoholics/addicts, or by members of their families—collected and edited by the host of the PBS-TV program *Late Night America*.

• **To Reach Many Non-AA "Anonymous" Organizations, and Non-AA Alcoholism/Addiction Recovery Organizations**
Internet links to the home pages on the World Wide Web for a great many organizations concerned with recovery from difficulties other than alcoholism/addiction are listed at the Web site titled "Online Recovery." More than forty of these organizations have adopted twelve-step programs patterned after the AA twelve-step program, and use *Anonymous* in the organizations's name. Listed as well are organizations sympathetic or supplemental to the AA program for adherents of different religions or for codependents of alcoholics/addicts.

Also listed at this Web site are organizations for recovery from alcoholism/addiction that differ from AA in their approach. None of these organizations is as large or as widely recognized for effectiveness as AA, but they obviously prove helpful for those to whom they appeal.

Web site: http://www.onlinerecovery.org

Another Internet Web site listing a large number and variety of twelve-step-inspired recovery programs (with Internet links to their Web sites) is titled "Sobriety and Recovery Resources." This information is given in the site's "Recovery Links" section. A number of other recovery-related sections are also available at this Web site, ranging from "Personal Stories & Articles" to "On-line AA meetings, chat channels, mailing lists" and "Recovery and Support Newsgroups."

Web site: http://www.recoveryresources.org

A similarly diverse Web site with links to many other sources but dealing only with alcoholism is titled "Another Empty Bottle."

Web site: http://www.alcoholismhelp.com

Chapter Two. The Professional Way: Intervention, Detox, Rehab, Aftercare

• *To Find Detox or Treatment Facilities Nearby*

Either AA or Al-Anon members should be able to tell you about detox-ification or treatment facilities in your area. In addition, persons at the AA information phone number given in your local telephone directory should also be able to inform you of nearby detoxes and treatment rehabs.

Or look in the yellow pages of a classified telephone directory for your locality. First, find such category listings as "Alcoholism Information and Treatment Centers" or "Drug Abuse and Addiction—Information and Treatment."

You can also be referred to detox or treatment facilities in your locale by phoning the following toll-free numbers (twenty-four hours a day, seven days a week), from anywhere in the country:

Alcohol and Drug Abuse Hotline: 1-800-729-6686 (a hotline operated by the U.S. Government)

National Drug and Alcohol Referral Hotline: 1-800-252-6465

Sources of Help and Information

• *Finding Treatment Facilities and Other Services Through a Special Organization*
You could in addition be referred to local detox or rehab treatment facilities
(as well as counseling services) in your locale through another nationwide
toll-free phone service. It is run by the National Council on Alcoholism and
Drug Dependence (NCADD), a nonprofit, voluntary federation of many
affiliate councils serving individual areas throughout the country. The
Council is one of America's largest and oldest private organizations providing help with alcoholism/addiction. The National Council's toll-free phone
number gives callers the local phone number of an affiliate council or treatment facility in the locale of the caller's postal ZIP code. Extensive information about alcoholism/addiction, prevention, counseling, and treatment
is also available from the Council and its affiliates.

> NCADD nationwide toll-free phone number: 1-800-NCA-CALL
> (1-800-622-2255)
> Mailing address: National Council on Alcoholism and Drug
> Dependence, 12 W. 21st Street, New York, NY 10010
> Phone: 212-206-6770
> Fax: 212-645-1690
> Web site: http://www.ncadd.org

• *You Could Also Search Out Detox/Rehab Treatment Programs on the Internet*
Instead of phoning the U.S. Hotline to find treatment programs, you
could access its entire national directory of such programs on the World
Wide Web. Its Web site address (URL) is: http://wwwdasis.samhsa.gov/
UFDS/welcome.htm.

(*Note: There is no period after the "www" in the above Web page address.
The lack of a period is NOT a typographical error.*)

This Web site will give you access to the complete and current listings—of some 11,300 treatment facilities throughout the United States
and its territories—in a directory also published as a book: *National Directory of Drug Abuse and Alcoholism Treatment Programs, 1998* (compiled
by the Office of Applied Studies, Substance Abuse and Mental Health
Services Administration, U.S. Department of Health and Human Services; Rockville, Md., 1999).

Sources of Help and Information

• *Finding a Counselor Skilled in Intervention*

You should be able to find a specialist in intervention by telephoning several of the treatment facilities for alcoholism/addiction in your area.

National Intervention Network: Sources of counseling help with an intervention are also available through the National Intervention Network of the National Council on Alcoholism and Drug Dependency. You can access such help through the following toll-free "hope"-line telephone number, the following Internet Web site, or the National Council's mailing address (given above).

Phone: 1-800-654-HOPE (1-800-654-4673)
Web site: http://www.ncadd.org/interven/html:

• *Books on Intervention*

Vernon E. Johnson, *I'll Quit Tomorrow* (New York: Harper & Row, 1973). The classic, original book on intervention as a technique to get an alcoholic/addict to begin recovery.

————, *Intervention—How to Help Someone Who Doesn't Want Help: A Step-By-Step Guide for Families and Friends of Chemically Dependent Persons* (Minneapolis, Minn.: Johnson Institute, 1986).

Johnson Institute, *Training Families to Do a Successful Intervention: A Professional's Guide* (Minneapolis, Minn.: Johnson Institute, 1996).

• *Books on Techniques in Therapy to Help an Alcoholic/Addict Begin Recovery*

William R. Miller and Stephen Rollnick, *Motivational Interviewing: Preparing People to Change Addictive Behavior* (New York: Guilford Press, 1991). The major book on this technique for use by professional therapists.

James O. Prochaska, et al., *Changing for Good* (New York: Avon Books, 1994). Explains a recently developed theory to bring about major personal and behavioral change in general; applications of the theory have begun proving effective in use by professional therapists seeking to help cocaine addicts, heroin addicts, and alcoholics begin recovery.

• *Books Concerning Treatment of Alcoholism/Addiction Generally*

Mim J. Landry, *Overview of Addiction Treatment Effectiveness* (Rockville,

Md.: Department of Health and Human Services, 1997). Presents an analytical summary of a great many research studies of the effectiveness of wide varieties of treatment for alcoholism/addiction, and finds in general that much research "substantiates the effectiveness of addiction treatment."

Office of Applied Studies, Substance Abuse and Mental Health Services Administration, *National Directory of Drug Abuse and Alcoholism Treatment Programs 1998* (Rockville, Md.: Department of Health and Human Services, 1999). A directory of more than eleven thousand state-approved treatment programs throughout the United States, giving basic information on each program. The contents of this directory can also be accessed on the World Wide Web (as noted near the start of this section on sources related to chapter 2).

Richard Ries, *Assessment and Treatment of Patients with Coexisting Mental Illness and Alcohol and Other Drug Abuse* (Rockville, Md.: U.S. Department of Health and Human Services, 1994). A work in the Treatment Improvement Protocol Series of the Department's Center for Substance Abuse Treatment, this book gives professionals practical information about treatment for alcoholics/addicts who also suffer from mental illnesses.

• *Special Sources for Publications and Research Information on Alcoholism/ Addiction and Recovery*

Readers wanting especially extensive publications or research information about alcoholism/addiction and recovery may find the major sources below helpful.

Hazelden Foundation: (Hazelden is a leading publisher in the field, issuing a great many books, booklets, and other materials. Hazelden also operates a number of treatment centers across the country, and conducts training and research programs.)

Mailing address: P.O. Box 11, CO3, Center City, MN 55012-0011
Phone: 1-800-257-7810, toll-free
Web site: www.hazelden.org

Sources of Help and Information

Rutgers University Center of Alcohol Studies: (The pioneer university research center for studies related to alcoholism and recovery. It led in the national movement to have the American Medical Association accept alcoholism as a treatable illness, a policy the AMA formally adopted in the 1950s. Today the center conducts research and training, and publishes a leading scholarly journal in the field.)
Web site: www.rci.rutgers.edu/~cas2

University of Washington Alcohol and Drug Abuse Institute Library: (More than seventy-five alcohol and drug abuse research centers are listed at this library. Most are at universities in the United States, but the list includes centers around the world. The library's Web site names and gives hypertext links for each center, providing access to each center's home page. Enormous amounts of information are thus available through this site. The research center listing represents only the first section of the Internet site's "category index" of the library. Other sections give similar listings and Internet access for U.S. government agencies, organizations and advocacy groups, other information resources, and international government agencies, professional societies, and journals and newsletters.)
Web site: http://depts.washington.edu/adai/links/catindex.htm (with links to research centers)

"Partnership for a Drug-Free America" for Information on Drugs and Prevention: (Reliable information on drugs and much information on preventing alcoholism/addiction is available through this well-known nonprofit organization dedicated to reducing demand for illegal drugs through media communication. Its Internet Web site notes that much drug information on the Internet is not accurate, but that the information on its site has been verified and is documented by sources given on the site.)

Mailing address: Partnership for a Drug-Free America, 405 Lexington Avenue, 16th Floor, New York, NY 10174
Phone: 212-922-1560
Web site: http://drugfreeamerica.org

Sources of Help and Information

American Society of Addiction Medicine: (Persons seeking extensive professional information on treatment for alcoholism/addiction—and on public issues concerning treatment—would find this organization helpful. It issues a quarterly journal of scholarly articles and other publications, and describes itself as "the nation's medical specialty society dedicated to educating physicians and improving the treatment of individuals suffering from alcoholism or other addictions." It certifies physicians in the specialty of addiction medicine. Abstracts of articles in its journal, and much other professional information, are available on its Web site. The site includes Web links to sources of much other related information.)

Mailing address: American Society of Addiction Medicine, Arcade Suite 101, 4601 North Park Avenue, Chevy Chase, MD 20815
Phone: 301-656-3920
Fax: 301-656-3815
Web site: http://www.asam.org

American Academy of Addiction Psychiatry: This membership organization for psychiatrists especially concerned with treatment of individuals suffering from addictions and mental illnesses is a major source of professional information in this area. It issues a quarterly journal of scholarly articles, a newsletter, and other publications. Its Web site includes Web links to other sites giving much additional related information.

Mailing address: American Academy of Addiction Psychiatry, 7301 Mission Road, Suite 252, Prairie Village, KS 66208
Phone: 913-262-6161
Fax: 913-262-4311
Web site: http://www.aaap.org

Extensive information—general, professional, and research information—at the Internet Web sites of two major U.S. government agencies:

Sources of Help and Information

Very extensive information about alcoholism/addiction for the general public, professionals providing treatment, and research specialists, is available at the Internet Web sites of two major agencies of the U.S. government in the field.

The National Institute on Alcohol Abuse and Alcoholism is one of these agencies.

Web site: http://www.niaaa.nih.gov

The National Institute on Drug Abuse is the other of the agencies.

Web site: http://www.nida.nih.gov

Chapter Three. The Al-Anon Way: To Stop Enabling; To Detach with Love

• *To Find Nearby Al-Anon Groups or the Central Office*

Al-Anon groups should be functioning right in your own community or neighborhood, or nearby. The most certain way to discover groups in your locale is by phoning the following toll-free numbers, or by using mail, fax, or the Internet.

Al-Anon Family Group Headquarters, Inc. (Al-Anon's World Service Office):

Telephone toll-free: In the United States, 1-888-425-2666 (1-888-4AL-ANON); in Spanish, 1-800-939-2770. In Canada, 1-800-443-4525.

Mailing address: 1600 Corporate Landing Parkway, Virginia Beach, VA 23454-5617, U.S.A.

Phone: 757-563-1600

Fax: 757-563-1655

Web site: http://www.al-anon.alateen.org

E-mail: wso@al-anon.org

• *Official Al-Anon Books*

Al-Anon Family Group Headquarters publishes and distributes numbers of books and pamphlets that are the official publications of the

Al-Anon program for relatives and friends of alcoholics, the Alateen program for teenage children of alcoholics, and Al-Anon's Adult Children program. All these publications are available from the Al-Anon Headquarters office. Many official books and pamphlets are often also available at meetings of Al-Anon groups. Among major Al-Anon books are the following.

Al-Anon Faces Alcoholism, 2d ed. (Virginia Beach, Va.: Al-Anon Family Group Headquarters, 1984). A first major part of this book presents articles by leading authorities who are "Those Who Work with the Problem," while a second major part presents short life stories by wide varieties of individuals who are "Those Who Live with the Problem."

Al-Anon Family Groups (Virginia Beach, Va.: Al-Anon Family Group Headquarters, 1966). The basic book about Al-Anon and the Al-Anon program.

Alateen—Hope for the Children of Alcoholics, (Virginia Beach Va.: Al-Anon Family Group Headquarters, 1973). The basic book of the Alateen program, which is for adolescent children of alcoholics. For them, the book treats alcoholism and the family, explains the Alateen program, and presents short life stories of adolescents in families of alcoholics.

• *Other Books (and an Internet Site) for Relatives or Friends of Alcoholics/Addicts*
Melanie Beattie, *Codependent No More: How to Stop Controlling Others and Start Caring for Yourself*, 2d ed. (Center City, Minn.: Hazelden, 1996). A classic work, widely used by family members of alcoholics/addicts for help with their recovery.

Claudia Black, *"It Will Never Happen to Me!"* (New York: Ballantine, 1987). A major book about and for children of alcoholics, as children and adults.

Children of Alcoholics Foundation. This nonprofit organization affiliated with Phoenix House provides educational materials and services "to help professionals, children, and adults break the intergenerational cycle of parental substance abuse." Its World Wide Web home page address is: http://www.coaf.org.

Ruth Maxwell, *The Booze Battle* (New York: Ballantine, 1977). A widely influential book to help those who live or work with an alcoholic, by a noted alcoholism counselor.

Sources of Help and Information

Arthur Wassmer, *Recovering Together: How to Help an Alcoholic Without Hurting Yourself* (New York: St. Martin's Press, 1989). Especially for spouses or other life-partners of alcoholics/addicts.

Janet Geringer Woititz, *Adult Children of Alcoholics* (Deerfield Beach, Fla.: Health Communications, 1990). Also a major book about and for the adult children of alcoholics.

Chapter Four. The Work-Life Way: Programs to Start Recovery for Employees or Professionals

• *For Employers, to Get Information About Employee Assistance Programs, or Federal Drug-Free Workplace Requirements*
You can call this "Workplace Helpline" operated by the U.S. Department of Health and Human Services as follows:

Phone: (toll-free) 1-800-WORKPLACE (1-800-967-5752)

• *To Find the International Doctors in AA Organization*
This organization of doctoral-level health-care professionals in AA can be reached as follows:

Mailing address: IDAA, P.O. Box 199, Augusta, MO 63332
Phone: 636-482-4548
Fax: 636-228-4102
Web site: http://members.aol.com/aadocs

• *To Find if a State Nurses Association Has a "Peer Assistance Program"*
State nurses associations need to be contacted individually to see if the association has a program to help nurses impaired by alcoholism/addiction. You can find out how to reach a state's nurses association from the American Nurses Association, as follows:

Mailing address: American Nurses Association, 600 Maryland Avenue, S.W., Washington, DC 20024-2571

Sources of Help and Information

Phone: (toll-free) 1-800-274-4ANA (1-800-274-4262)
Web sites: http://www.ana.org/snaweb.htm and http://www.ana.org/snaaddr.htm

- **To Find the International Nurses Anonymous Organization**

This organization of nurses in AA can be reached as follows:

Mailing address: International Nurses Anonymous, 1020 Sunset Drive, Lawrence, KS 66044
Phone: 913-842-3893
Web site: http://www.crml.uab.edu/~jah/ina.html:

- **To Find Information About a Lawyer Assistance Program**

You can obtain information about a Lawyer Assistance Program for a possible alcoholic/addict lawyer you know from the following source:

Mailing address: Commission on Lawyer Assistance Programs, American Bar Association, 541 N. Fairbanks Court, Chicago, IL 60611
Phone: 312-988-5522
Web site: http://www.abanet.org/cpr/colap/home.html:

- **To Find Out About Help in Starting Recovery for an Airline Pilot**

You can inquire about programs to help an alcoholic/addict airline pilot start recovery by telephoning the Employee Assistance Program at the main offices of the airline for which the pilot works. Or you can do so with the Air Line Pilots Association.

Air Line Pilots Association: Mailing address: Human Resources Department, Air Line Pilots Association, P.O. Box 1169, Herndon, VA 20172
Phone and Fax: 703-464-2110
E-mail: humanresources@alpa.org

Sources of Help and Information

- *Publications on Helping Employees or Professionals Start Recovery from Alcoholism/Addiction*

Robert Holman Coombs, *Drug-Impaired Professionals* (Cambridge, Mass.: Harvard University Press, 1997). A unique, extensive study.

James M. Oher, ed., *The Employee Assistance Handbook* (New York: Wiley, 1999). A guide to virtually all aspects of starting and operating an Employee Assistance Program for an employing organization.

Substance Abuse and Mental Health Administration, *Making Your Workplace Drug Free: A Kit for Employers, Employer Tip Sheet #10* (Rockville, Md.: Department of Health and Human Services, no date). A three-pocket portfolio of booklets, folders, and posters for employing organizations. Available free on request to the toll-free phone number, 1-800-WORKPLACE.

Carol Cox Smith, *Recovery at Work: A Clean and Sober Career Guide* (San Francisco: Harper & Row/Hazelden, 1990). A comprehensive guide for individual alcoholics/addicts starting recovery on how to solve any problems that arise in connection with either employment or professional work.

———, *Turning Problem Employees into Successes: A Handbook for Managers and Supervisors* (Minneapolis, Minn.: Johnson Institute, 1992). Explains in practical detail how managers and supervisors can deal effectively with employees of theirs who are alcoholics/addicts.

Jeffrey Lynn Speller, *Executives in Crisis: Recognizing and Managing the Alcoholic, Drug-Addicted, or Mentally Ill Executive* (San Francisco: Jossey-Bass, 1989). Tells how organizations can solve a wide range of problems caused by alcoholic/addict executives.

Chapter Five. The Law-Enforcement Way: Drunk-Driving Arrests, Drug Courts, Prison Programs

- *To Obtain Information About Drunk Driving*

You can obtain information about all aspects of drunk driving as follows:

Mothers Against Drunk Driving, MADD: *Web site:* http://www.madd.org

Sources of Help and Information

• *To Obtain Information About Drug Courts*
You can access extensive information about the Drug Courts Program of the U.S. Department of Justice as follows:
Web site: http://ojp.usdoj.gov/home.htm

Chapter Six. The Therapeutic-Community Way: Daytop, Phoenix House, Samaritan, Others

• *To Obtain Information About Daytop Village Programs*
Information on the many programs of the Daytop Village organization (usually called simply Daytop) can be obtained from its toll-free telephone hotline, which is:

Phone: (toll-free) 1-800-2-DAYTOP (1-800-232-9867), or 212-354-6000
Mailing address: Daytop Village, Inc., 54 W. 40th Street, New York, NY 10018
Web site: http://www.daytop.org

• *To Obtain Information on Phoenix House Programs and on Other Therapeutic-Community Programs in Your Locale*
Information on Phoenix House programs, and referrals to local therapeutic-community programs and other types of treatment and assistance, is available at all times from the following Phoenix House Foundation hotline:

Phone: (toll-free) 1-800-DRUGHELP (1-800-378-4435)
(Crisis intervention help with referrals to local sources of crisis services for alcoholics/addicts is also a main function of this DRUGHELP hotline.)
Web site: http://www.phoenixhouse.org
Phoenix House mailing address, e-mail address, and telephone number: Phoenix Houses of New York, Jack R. Aron Center, 164 W. 74th Street, New York, NY 10023; (e-mail) phcomm@phoenixhouse.org; (phone) 212-595-5810.

Sources of Help and Information

(*Note*: Five more Phoenix Houses executive offices are located in California, Texas, Florida, Long Island (New York), and New England. Their addresses are available from the New York City office or the Phoenix House Web site.)

• To Obtain Other Referrals to Therapeutic-Community Treatment Programs
You could also obtain referrals to therapeutic-community programs in your vicinity through the following Alcohol and Drug Abuse Hotline of the U.S. government (given also in chapter 2):
Phone: (toll-free) 1-800-729-6686

• Books on Therapeutic Communities
Essie E. Lee, *Breaking the Connection: How Young People Achieve Drug-Free Lives* (New York: Simon & Schuster/Julian Messner, 1988). Includes extensive reports on the pioneer therapeutic-community treatment organizations, Daytop Village and Phoenix House.

David Kennard, *An Introduction to Therapeutic Communities*, 2d ed. (London: Jessica Kingsley, 1998). A wide-ranging and informative report on the origins and workings of therapeutic communities in the United States as well as in Great Britain, dealing with communities for the mentally ill as well as those for alcoholics/addicts.

Msr. William B. O'Brien and Ellis Henican, *You Can't Do It Alone: The Daytop Way to Make Your Child Drug-Free* (New York: Simon & Schuster, 1993). A detailed account of the founding, growth, and wide influence of the Daytop Village organization.

Epilogue: Essentials/Safeguards for Staying in Recovery

• To Obtain Information About the AA-Oriented High Watch Farm
You or your alcoholic/addict can get in touch with High Watch Farm (the recovery residential community traditionally very close to AA) as follows:

Mailing address: High Watch Farm, P.O. Box 607, Kent, CT 06757
Phone: (toll-free) 1-888-HWF-KENT (1-888-493-5368), or 860-927-3772
Web site: http://www.highwatchfarm.com

Sources of Help and Information

• *To Obtain Information About the Oxford House Recovery Residential Communities*

Mailing address: Oxford House, Inc., ICA Group Foundation, P.O. Box 994, Great Falls, VA 22066-0994
Phone: (toll-free) 1-800-486-6488, or 703-450-6501
Fax: (toll-free) 1-800-899-6577, or 703-450-6577
TTY (TDD) Service for the Deaf: 703-450-6503
Web site: http://www.icagroup.org/main.html

• *Books on Maintaining Continued Recovery from Alcoholism/Addiction*

Anne Geller, *Restore Your Life: A Living Plan for Sober People* (New York: Bantam, 1991). A physician and former director of the widely known Smithers Alcoholism Treatment Center in New York City draws on rich professional experience to tell how to protect sobriety.

L. Ann Mueller and Katherine Ketcham, *Recovering: How to Get and Stay Sober* (New York: Bantam, 1987). The third part of this comprehensive guide provides most helpful guidance on "staying sober" through the early, middle, and late stages of recovery.

Living Sober: Some Methods A.A. Members Have Used for Not Drinking (New York: Alcoholics Anonymous World Services, 1975). A highly readable set of short articles describing many of the most effective, time-proven ways in which AA members safeguard their recovery.

Index

AA

Alcoholics Anonymous as basic book in, 19;
Alcoholics Anonymous World Services,
Inc., phone numbers/addresses, 193–194;
anonymity in, 40–41; basic actions in to
achieve recovery, 35–41; co-founders
Bill W. and Dr. Bob S., 36; drug addicts
widely welcomed by AA groups, 21;
effectiveness of AA-oriented treatment
programs, 89–90; evaluations of AA
effectiveness by outside experts, 23–24;
finding detox or rehab treatment
facilities through, 198; founding date (6/
10/35), 36; General Service Office, 41;
getting a sponsor in, 38–39; getting help
from in a crisis, 13–14; groups for
lawyers in, 139; groups of in all U.S./
Canadian locales, 13; HALT acronym
to promote recovery, 175; High Watch
Farm as special group residence, 178–
179; High Watch Farm phone numbers/
addresses, 210; how to find detox
through, 15; how to find local groups of,
12–13, 193–194; how to reach General
Service Office of (for U.S. and Canada),
193–194; joining a group in, 38; major
official publications of, 195–196; major
unofficial books about, 196; meetings in
prisons, 154; meetings of open to
nonalcoholics, 17; members' experience
with death due to alcoholism/addiction,
166; membership requirement of, 17;
numbers of AA groups, 13, 42; numbers
of AA members, 11, 42; oil-rigs
roustabout example of member life-story,
27–31; "one day at a time" slogan and
its uses, 35–36; openness to other ways
of recovery, 42; organization for nurses
in, 137; phone numbers/addresses for

International Doctors in AA, 206;
physicians organization in, 134–135;
regal beauty example of AA member life-
story, 31–35; required attendance of as
imprisonment alternative, 143; sayings
about alcoholism/addiction as a disease,
166; spirituality in, 109; statistics on
members' years of sobriety, 42; test
questions for alcoholism from, 6–8; the
twelve steps of, 110; tools used in to
fight off cravings for alcohol/drugs, 30;
12th-Step "carrying the message," 37;
"12th-Step" help with crises, 14;
12th-step work to counter complacence,
176; twelve-step support groups similar
to, 22–23; typical hours at which
meetings held, 18; unique character of,
40–41; view of alcoholism/addiction as a
disease within, 165–166; views in on
dangers of the first drink, 168; Web sites
for on-line AA meetings and diverse AA
information, 194
abstinence, difficulty in understanding need
for in recovery, 167; essential for
recovery, 167
Adcare Hospital, Worcester, MA, 56
addiction medicine (physicians'
subspecialty), xiii, 64
addiction to both alcohol and drugs, xii
addictive prescription drugs, xii
adult children of alcoholics, Al-Anon
Family Group for, 101
aftercare, in therapeutic community
programs, 160; planning for following
rehab, 82–83
Air Line Pilots Association, addresses/
phone numbers, 141, 207; recovery
programs role, 140
airline pilots, *see* pilots

Index

Al-Anon's Adult Children, part of Al-Anon for adult children of alcoholics, 101;

Al-Anon
Al-Anon Family Group Headquarters phone numbers/addresses, 96–97; 204; Alateen as part of, 101; as companion body to AA, 12; as means for helping start recovery, 92–95; confidentiality in, 99; detach with love as vital action for a member, 116–118; effects on starting an alcoholic/addict in recovery, 118–119; ending enabling of the alcoholic/addict, 94; finding local meetings of, 96–97; greater (or higher) power in, 113; guaranteed promise of, 119; helpful effects of first step in, 112–113; helpful to those involved with drug addicts, 100–101; home group in, 103; hostility toward by an alcoholic/addict, 102; *How Al-Anon Works for Families and Friends of Alcoholics*, 118; how steps in help curb enabling, 114–115; importance of persisting in, 102; numbers of groups of, 98; official publications of, 204–205; recommended in family treatment, 88; recovery in for a member, 105–106; relief brought by steps in, 115–116; role in recognizing alcoholism/addiction, 94–95; role in recovery for family members, 94–95; second step in, 113; selecting a group to join, 97–98; slogans in, 106–109; spirit-quality in, 108–109; sponsor in, 104–105; steps in for making amends, 116–117; text of the twelve steps in, 111–112; the twelve steps of, 109–118; typical character of meetings and members, 98–100; using for a social support group, 184; value of when the alcoholic/addict starts recovery, 120; World Service Office, 96–97

Alcohol and Drug Abuse Hotline (of U.S. government), 56

Alcoholics Anonymous (AA basic book), 19, 39

Alcoholics Anonymous, *see* AA

alcoholics, number in U.S., xii

alcoholism/addiction
AA test questions for, 6–8; abstinence needed for recovery from, 167; brain chemistry changes resulting from, 167–168; confidentiality in treatment of, 51–52; denial in, xiii, xiv; effect on work-life of an alcoholic/addict, 121; effects on family members, 92–93; fatal as a disease, 166; getting AA help in a crisis of, 13–14; hideous end if unchecked, 19; incurable as a disease, 166; large role in crime, 153; major books on for relatives/friends of alcoholics/addicts, 205–206; major sources for research findings on, 201–204; medical recognition of as a disease, xiii; medically termed chemical dependence or substance abuse, xiii; physical predisposition for, 4; priority of in treating mental illness, 172–173; professional help in a crisis of, 43–45; progressive as a disease, 166; return to recovery after a relapse to, 177; major books about, 196–197; special horror of as a disease, 108; substance abuse vs. chemical dependence, 129–130; symptoms used by psychiatrists to diagnose, 8–10; withdrawal dangers when stopping, 15–16

American Academy of Addiction Psychiatry, 203–204

American Bar Association, addresses/phone numbers, 139; Commission on Lawyer Assistance Programs, 138; recovery programs report, 137

American Medical Association, resolution on alcoholic/addict physicians, 132–133

American Nurses Association, addicted nurses policy, 135; addresses/phone numbers, 136, 206

American Society of Addiction Medicine, 203; Patient Placement Criteria of, 64

Amity, prison treatment program in California, 156

anesthesia, precautions with to safeguard recovery, 170

Index

Antabuse to counter alcohol cravings, 84–85

Arizona, special state drug courts program of, 149–150

attorneys, *see* lawyers

BAC, *see* blood alcohol content

barbiturates, 170

Betty Ford Center for treating alcoholism/addiction, 2

Bill W. (AA co-founder), 36

bipolar disorder, 171

blackout, defined, 6

blood alcohol content, amounts needed for coma/death, 145; minimum amounts for DUI/DWI, 145; relation to number of drinks consumed, 145

Bob S., Dr. (AA co-founder), 36

brain chemistry changes, resulting from alcoholism/addiction, 167–168

Breathalyzer, use in DUI/DWI convictions, 145

Brighton Hospital, 134

CA, as a parallel body to AA, 22; meetings in prisons, 154; World Services Office, phone numbers/addresses for, 194–195

California, state actions on drug courts, 150–151

Carter, President Jimmy, 1

celebrities and alcoholism/addiction, 1–2

Center for Substance Abuse Prevention (U.S. government), 126

Chase, Chevy, actor, 2

Cheever, Susan, author, 2

chemical dependence as medical term for alcoholism/addiction, xiii; how differs from substance abuse, 129–130

Clinton, President Bill, 1

Cocaine Anonymous, *see* CA

confidentiality, in treatment programs, 51–52; of professionals in recovery programs, 132; in EAPs, 127

consultants, for EAPs, 124

Cornerstone, prison treatment program in Oregon, 156

cost, California savings from drug courts, 151; N.Y.S. drug courts savings, 152; of alcohol/drug abuse to businesses in U.S., 123; of imprisonment versus treatment, 154

costs, in therapeutic community programs, 163; of types of treatment, 90–91

crime, large role of alcoholism/addiction in, 153

crisis, getting help in a, 13–14, 43–45

Dade County Circuit Court, 148–149

dangers to someone close to an alcoholic/addict, xiv, xiv

Daytop Village, founding, 163; how to contact, 160–161; long-term success rate, 164; numbers recovering through, 163; phone numbers/addresses, 209

death, alcohol consumption level that results in, 145; as end of unchecked alcoholism/addiction, 19; from alcoholism/addiction in AA members' experience, 166

Dederich, Charles (Synanon founder), 163

Delaware, Key-Crest Program for treatment in prisons, 154–155

denial in alcoholism/addiction, xiii, xiv; power of, 13; in hostility against Al-Anon, 102–103; work as the last fortress of, 121

depression, 171

detach with love, as vital action for an Al-Anon member, 116–118; importance of, 183–184

detox, basic elements in, 15; desirable features of, 74–75; finding facility for in advance, 44–45; how to find through AA, 15; in an emergency, 45; inpatient or outpatient, 52–53; inpatient program character, 75–77; need for, 15, 44, 70–71; outpatient program character, 77–78

detoxification treatment or program, *see* detox

Dexedrine, 170

Diagnostic and Statistical Manual of Mental Disorders, Fourth Edition, 8

Index

disease recognition of alcoholism/addiction by physicians, xiii

doctors, *see* physicians

driving under the influence, as common reason for police arrests, 142; breath or urine tests for, 144–145

driving while intoxicated, as reason for police arrests, 142; diversion to treatment after conviction of, 146; effect of multiple convictions of, 146; penalties for conviction of, 146

drug addicts, drug court rehabilitation services for, 148; number in U.S., xii; widely welcomed by AA groups, 21

Drug Courts Program (of U.S. Dept. of Justice), 143; origin, 149; Web site for, 208

drug courts, advantages of Arizona program of, 150; California savings from, 151; California state actions on, 150–151; requirements imposed on addicts, 148; N.Y.S. actions on, 150–151; origins of, 148–149; rehabilitation services for addicts, 148; special Arizona program of, 149–150; statistics on extent, 149; successful recovery rates of, 148; typical experience of addicts with, 147–148; Web site for major information source on, 208

drug testing, by hair or breath sample, 131–132; by urine sample, 130; of employees, 130–132

Drug-Free Workplace Act (U.S. statute), 125

drug-free workplace, toll-free U.S. Government number for information on, 206; U.S. government agencies' requirements for, 125; "Workplace Help Line" phone number, 125

drunk driving, high fatalities rate of, 144; jail sentences for, 144; numbers arrested for annually, 144; Web site for major information source on, 208 DSM-IV symptoms for alcoholism/addiction, 8–10

dual diagnosis (of alcoholism/addiction and mental illness), 62–64

DUI, *see* driving under the influence

DWI, *see* driving while intoxicated

EAPs, conduct of typical case in, 126–130; confidentiality protection in, 127; employee confrontation in, 128; employee drug testing in, 131; for nurses, 136–137; for pilots, 140; getting recovery started through, 123–124; how available for small firms, 124; outside consultants for, 124; protection of employee rights in, 126; difficulties addressed by, 122–123; role in starting recovery, 122; substance abusers in, 129–130; supervisor or other case-compiler role in, 126–128; supervisor training for, 127; toll-free U.S. Government number for information on, 206; *Turning Problem Employees into Successes*, 126

"easy does it," as Al-Anon slogan, 107

emergencies, preparing for, 184

employee assistance programs, *see* EAPs

employees, major books/publications on helping impaired, 207–208

enabling, how Al-Anon steps help curb, 114–115; importance of ending, 94, 183

family members, effects of alcoholism/addiction on, 92–93

family treatment for relatives of alcoholics/addicts, 88–89

Federal Aviation Administration, recovery programs role, 140

"first things first," as Al-Anon slogan, 106–107

First, Dr. Michael B., 23

Fisher, Carrie, actor, 2

Ford, First Lady Betty, 1

Ford, President Gerald, 1

Frances, Dr. Allen, 23

Gamblers Anonymous (GA), 23

Gordon, Barbara, TV producer, 2

halfway house residence to bolster recovery, 83

Index

Index

physicians, American Medical Association resolution on addicted, 132–133; organization for in AA, 134–135; recovery programs for, 132–135

pilots, factors causing start in recovery, 140; license retention through recovery programs, 140; phone number/addresses to get help for impaired, 207; recovery programs for, 141

Presidents (U.S.), and alcoholism/addiction in families of, 1

prison, *see* imprisonment

professionals, Web site for special groups of in recovery, 193; major books on helping impaired, 207–208; types of having recovery programs, 122, 132

Project MATCH study of treatment types effectiveness, 89–90

psychiatrists, symptoms used by for diagnosing alcoholism/addiction, 8–10

recovery needs of someone close to an alcholic/addict, xv, xvi

recovery
"hitting bottom" as the cause for starting on, 18–20; AA approach of one day at a time, 169; AA tools used to fight off cravings for alcohol/drugs, 30; AA twelfth-step work to counter complacence in, 176; AA's HALT acronym to promote, 175; absolute abstinence essential for, 167; Al-Anon as means for helping start, 92–95; Al-Anon role in for family members, 94–95; Al-Anon value when the alcoholic/addict starts, 120; American Bar Association recovery programs report, 137; basic actions in AA to achieve, 35–41; bolstered by changing actions, 175; bolstered by frequent meetings, 174–175; bolstered by longevity in treatment, 84; complacence as threat to, 176; counseling techniques to help start, 65–70; couples therapy to help start, 69–70; EAPs to help start, 122; effects of altered brain chemistry in, 173–174;

factors causing pilots' recovery start, 140; helpful family-member actions in, 180–181; fostered in AA by members' help, 36–37; getting started through EAPs, 123–124; halfway house residence to bolster, 83; high success rate with longevity in any program, 164; how employee drug testing could start, 132; importance of prompt return to after a relapse, 177; imprisonment as motivation to start, 143; intervention as professional method to start, 45–46; major books on for relatives/friends of alcoholics/addicts, 205–206; major books on maintaining continued, 211; major books on therapy techniques for helping start, 200–201; major sources for research findings on, 201–204; need for medical checkup at start of, 16; need for vigilance in, 173–174; network therapy technique to help start, 65, 67–69; numbers recovering through AA, 11; numbers starting through therapeutic community programs, 164; of person close to an alcoholic/addict, 182–183; Oxford House residential communities phone numbers/addresses, 211; police arrests as motivation to start, 142; power of AA member life-stories to initiate start of, 25–27; precautions with anesthesia to safeguard, 170; precautions with medications to safeguard , 169–171; precautions with mouthwashes to safeguard, 170; precautions with nonprescription drugs in, 170; programs for lawyers. 137–139; programs for nurses, 135–137; programs for persons in religious vocations, 141; programs for physicians, 132–135; promoted by mental-illness drugs if prescribed, 171–172; relapse triggered by any alcohol/drug use, 168; results of Ohio lawyer assistance program, 138; rewards of, xvii; safeguarding if addictive drugs are medically necessary, 171; satisfactions of attested by AA members, 166–167;

Index

Index

alternative, 143; basic elements in detox, 15; basic goal of in therapeutic community programs, 160; costs covered by health-insurance programs, xiii; characteristics in therapeutic community programs, 158–160; clients most suited for therapeutic community programs, 157; cognitive/behavioral programs effectiveness, 89–90; confidentiality protection in, 51–52; costs of types of, 90–91; counseling techniques to help start recovery, 65–70; couples therapy to help start recovery, 69–70; Delaware prisons Key-Crest Program, 154–155; desirable program features, 58–59; diversion to after multiple DWI convictions, 146; effect of court-mandated on recovery start, 146–147; effect on recovery of longevity in, 84; effectiveness findings in landmark study, 89–90; effectiveness of prison programs, 156; finding and selecting programs of, 55–64; finding detox or rehab facilities through AA, 198; for alcoholics/addicts with added mental illness, 62–64; for family members of alcoholics/addicts, 88; how to find detox through AA, 15; importance of for family members, 184; major books about intervention, 200; major books on therapy techniques for helping start recovery, 200–201; medicines to counter alcohol/drug cravings, 85–86; motivational enhancement programs effectiveness, 89–90; motivational interviewing technique in, 65–67; need for medical checkup at recovery start, 16; network therapy technique in, 65, 67–69; number of programs in prisons, 156; Patient Placement Criteria in, 64; possible need for repeated exposures to, 185; private

hotline for referrals to programs of, 56; 198; programs available during imprisonment, 154–156; programs for heroin addicts, 86–87; therapeutic community type in prisons, 154; type of programs, 52–55; U.S. directory listings of San Jose, CA, programs, 58, 60–63; U.S. Government hotline for referrals to programs of, 56, 198; U.S. Government Web site for finding detox/rehab facilities, 57, 199

Turning Problem Employees into Successes, 126

Twelfth-Step help from AA in crises, 14, 37

twelve steps, of AA and Al-Anon, 109–110; text of in Al-Anon, 111–112

twelve-step support groups similar to AA, 22–23; Web sites for, 197–198

University of Washington Alcohol and Drug Abuse Institute Library, 202

Vaillant, Dr. George E., 24
Valium, 169, 170

Welch, Bob, baseball star, 2
withdrawal reactions as addiction driving force, 70; dangers of when stopping alcoholism/addiction, 15–16; detox needed to counteract safely, 70–71; duration, 71, 79; from alcohol, 71–72; from crack, cocaine, or speed, 73; from hallucinogens, 74; from inhalants, 74; from marijuana, 74; from narcotics like heroin, 72; from tranquilizers or sedative drugs, 73; torture of, 70

work, role of in starting/blocking recovery, 121

Your Mental Health, evaluation of AA effectiveness in, 23–24